PLAYING THE LONG GAME

PLAYING THE LONG GAME

A MEMOIR

CHRISTINE SINCLAIR
WITH STEPHEN BRUNT

RANDOM HOUSE CANADA

PUBLISHED BY RANDOM HOUSE CANADA

Copyright © 2022 Christine Sinclair

www.penguinrandomhouse.ca

Random House Canada and colophon are registered trademarks.

LIBRARY AND ARCHIVES CANADA CATALOGUING IN PUBLICATION

Title: Playing the long game / Christine Sinclair, Stephen Brunt.
Names: Sinclair, Christine, 1983– author. | Brunt, Stephen, author.
Identifiers: Canadiana (print) 20220225079 | Canadiana (ebook) 20220226547
| ISBN 9781039004603 (hardcover) | ISBN 9781039004610 (EPUB)
Subjects: LCSH: Sinclair, Christine, 1983– | LCSH: Soccer players—Biography.
| LCSH: Women soccer players—Biography. | LCGFT: Autobiographies.
Classification: LCC GV942.7.S56 P53 2022 | DDC 796.334092—dc23

Text design: Matthew Flute
Jacket design: Matthew Flute
Image credits: (crowd) gnagel / iStock / Getty Images;
(Christine Sinclair) SOPA Images / Contributor / Getty Images

Printed in the United States of America

2 4 6 8 9 7 5 3 1

Penguin
Random House
RANDOM HOUSE CANADA

*This book is dedicated to my inspiration,
my mother, Sandra Sinclair. The strongest person
I have ever known, and the reason I am where I am
today. You won't get the chance to read this,
but I hope to continue to make you proud.
I love you and will miss you forever.*

CONTENTS

*Talking about myself has never
been something I've liked to do.*

For anyone who has followed my career, that won't come as a surprise. But I've lived the life of a female athlete. I've helped blaze some trails. I've gone from playing in front of maybe a hundred soccer fans to having an audience of millions. You've watched me drop to my knees in defeat and run around the pitch with my arms spread from the sheer thrill of the game. And if there ever was a right time—an opening to push for change, an opportunity to eradicate the fake distinction between women's and men's sports—the time is now.

So I'm talking. About my career. About what's at stake. Hoping that a whole new world will open for the young female athletes coming up. Hoping for a different world for my nieces, in sports or out.

1

"WE'RE CHANGING THE COLOUR OF THE MEDAL"

Looking back, I think we were perfectly built for a pandemic Olympics.

The thing that has always separated the Canadian women's national soccer team from other teams is how close we are, how connected we are, how much we enjoy each other's company. Athletes like to talk about how they have a great team culture. Ours is unique, in my experience, and not just the most recent version. It's a culture that was built over the years. During the pandemic, when we were locked in our hotels or the Olympic Village and couldn't even grab a coffee together at Starbucks, we could still rely on each other. We thrived on that.

When the COVID-19 lockdowns hit in March 2020, we were playing in the Tournoi de France. Things were going well—we lost to France, beat Holland, tied Brazil— and it felt like we were on track to have a good Olympics in Tokyo that summer. But the world changed over the course of those few days. The tournament went from completely normal, with fans in the stands, to no fans and no handshakes by the end. I remember our team doctor saying that he didn't think COVID was going to be that big of a deal and that everyone was making more of it than they should. The next thing you know we were being told to get out of Paris as fast as we could before we were trapped there.

The day after we flew home, the NBA shut down—and you know the rest.

I spent the first month of the pandemic in Florida. I had planned to go there on the way back from France to visit some friends before the start of the National Women's Soccer League (NWSL) pre-season. It was maybe not the safest place to be, given the lack of restrictions. Gyms closed for two weeks and then they reopened and everyone acted like COVID was over. I was hearing stories of teammates back in Canada who couldn't leave their houses and thinking that I had it pretty good there in the sun.

But then I went home to Portland, Oregon, and things got real.

As an athlete you are on a set schedule. You know exactly what you're doing tomorrow and the next day. Everything is planned out for you. But in the middle of the pandemic, we had to give up on that. Everything was changing so quickly. We had to let go of expectations and learn to accept that, for the time being, there were far more important things on this planet than kicking a ball around.

All our players were isolated, and all the clubs were shut down. But we chose to make the most of it. As a team we were going to use every day in the hopes that there would still be an Olympics. Our goal was to train more efficiently and effectively than our opponents despite the obstacles. We weren't going let a lack of games and a lack of normal preparation become an excuse.

Our strength and conditioning coach had us doing workouts together on Zoom. Desiree Scott ran a virtual Zumba class. All of us had our own homemade gyms where we could work out as best we could with whatever equipment was available. Mine was in my garage.

And then Canada pulled out of the Olympics.

I had the same reaction I'm sure a lot of athletes had: *What? Really? There is going to be an Olympics and Canada is not going? I've trained my whole life for this. If there is going to be an Olympics, they're going to do it safely. Shouldn't we be part of it?*

But within a day or two it became clear that the 2020 Games were going to be postponed for everyone.

That was at the end of March. In June, our coach, Kenneth Heiner-Møller, stepped down to take a job in Denmark, his home country. We understood. It was the right move for him and his family. His contract with the Canadian Soccer Association (CSA) ran through the Olympics, and now there weren't going to be any Olympics, at least not in 2020. He had been offered his dream job. It all made sense, but it meant that we no longer had a coach. As it turned out, we wouldn't have one for a long time.

My club team, the Portland Thorns of the National Women's Soccer League, returned to training around that time to prepare for the Challenge Cup, the first "bubble" event in professional sports. It was "distanced" training. Everyone got their own little square on the field, trying to prepare to play as a team at a time when we couldn't go near other people.

Still, we were proud that the NWSL was the first professional sports league to come back and play. We were the guinea pigs, and the league made it work. We showed that it could be done, and safely.

The tournament was held in July in Salt Lake City, Utah. It was one of those situations where you had to go in with an open mind and roll with it—and stay grateful just to have the opportunity to play and compete when everything else was still shut down.

Our team lived in a hotel in Salt Lake City for three and a half weeks. We couldn't leave the building except to go to practice or games, and though the food wasn't the greatest, the organizers did their best to make us comfortable. We had a massive games room with foosball and

Ping-Pong and a basketball hoop, but being isolated was still hard for players who hadn't experienced anything like it before. I've been travelling with the national team since I was sixteen and have been away from home for months at a time, so I adapted more easily than some of my teammates. We played well, but lost in the semi-finals.

After the tournament, I went home to Portland and things went quiet for quite a while. That fall there was a moment when we wondered whether we were ever going to get a head coach. There's only so much a team can do when its players aren't together, but if we had a coach we could at least start.

Diana Matheson had been playing with the national team almost as long as I had. Together, we called the Canadian Soccer Association and told them that the team was starting to stress. They asked for our opinions on what we wanted in a head coach—not for recommendations of individual people, but more generally. We said that we couldn't have a coach that had to start from scratch. There just wasn't enough time to hire someone who didn't know anybody and didn't know the program.

A week later that they named Bev Priestman as the new head coach. I don't think many people were surprised. Bev had been involved with our program as an assistant under John Herdman, who coached us from 2011 to 2018. She had also been the head coach of the youth national team, so she knew the athletes, knew how we had been playing, knew the language we used on the field.

The first word that pops into my mind when I think about Bev is *energy*: she is a *ball* of energy. But we could also tell that she had changed during her time working with the English women's national team; she'd accepted that job after John moved on to coach Canada's men and Kenneth took over our team. She was a more commanding coach than she had been. You could tell from the way she went about the work that John had had an impact on her—John generally does have a big impact on people. Compared to Bev, John is a little more black-and-white with tactics. With him, you play three different formations and know exactly what to do and where to go. Bev likes our game to be a bit more free-flowing, and she puts more emphasis on the players figuring it out for ourselves. John really focused on individual players at a deep level, connecting with each of us and getting the most out of us. With only seven or eight months before the rescheduled Olympics, Bev approached us as more of a collective, sparking a team conversation—with time so short, she had to get us to perform.

Right off the bat, though, she understood our strengths and let us play to them instead of trying to make us play a style that didn't fit our personnel. As a coach, that was the biggest difference between her and Kenneth. He'd tried to get us to play a more possession-oriented game, and it never really worked. We are a world-class defensive team that doesn't give up many big goals and thrives on the counterattack.

We were primed to have a good tournament based on age, experience and the mix of younger players with veteran players. As a team, in London in 2012 and Rio in 2016, we had really nailed down the Olympic tournament format, where there are such short breaks between games. And Bev also set a clear goal right from our very first meeting. She said, "We're changing the colour of the medal."

Bronze in London. Bronze in Rio. Now we were shooting for the top of the podium.

Would we have won the gold if Kenneth had stayed as our coach? Would it have gone the same way if the Olympics had happened on time and Bev hadn't come in? Who knows?

The first time we came back together in person as a team was in February 2021 at the SheBelieves Cup in Orlando. I couldn't be there because I had fractured my heel in training. I wasn't the only one missing: some of our key players were with their professional teams in France, and they weren't allowed to come to the United States because of COVID travel restrictions.

I talked to Bev a couple of days before the first game, which was against the United States. She asked me, "What do you think the team needs me to say?"

I told her not to worry about it: "You're playing the Americans. The team will show up." Our biggest rivals, the US team always seemed to be able to pull out a win, and basically pressed all of our buttons. Our team did show up—and I was so proud of them. Yes, we lost 1–0, but we played really well.

You could already see the difference Bev was making in our attitude and style. The players were less concerned about possession and more concerned about defending, and then about being dangerous on the counterattack. They weren't keeping the ball just for the sake of keeping the ball.

One of the players I especially noticed at that tournament was Vanessa Gilles. Her journey to the national team is a prime example of why Canada needs a women's professional league. Instead of playing at home, Vanessa was playing in France, both on a professional team and for the French U23 national team, which she could do because her dad was born in France and she has a French passport. Under Kenneth, she finally started to get called up to Canada's national team, but she never really got a chance on the field.

Under Bev, Vanessa soon developed into one of the best centre backs in the world. So many players like her just slip through the cracks or end up quitting the game because there is nowhere to play at home.

The next time the team got together was for a small tournament in England. That was a real turning point. We beat England and Wales—the 2–0 win over England was especially big, because they are one of the best teams in the world. If anyone hadn't yet bought into the new style we were playing, that game proved we were moving in the right direction.

For our last pre-Olympic matches, we went to Spain, where we played Brazil and the Czechs, and tied both.

You could see our team turning into what it would become in Tokyo.

Just before heading to Japan, we had a final camp in Los Angeles. It was a lot of fun—our last bit of freedom before moving into the Olympic bubble. We trained hard, and we went to the beach.

We had already heard some horror stories about what it was going to be like when we got off the plane in Japan. A group of Canadian athletes who had gone before us told us they were in the airport for six hours getting through protocols. We were prepared for the worst, but it wasn't too bad—three hours of getting tested and getting our accreditation. But from the moment we left the airport, I could tell that this wasn't going to be an Olympics like anything I had experienced before.

Our first matches were in Sapporo. There were no signs. There was no welcome. There was limited fanfare. It felt like large chunks of the Japanese population didn't want the Olympics to be happening.

The host country went to incredible lengths to keep us separated from the general public, to make sure that no one from the women's football tournament was going to give COVID to anybody on the outside. We went through back doors to enter the hotel. We used a separate elevator. There were workers in the elevator to make sure we only went to our floor and didn't go to any others. We didn't see anyone. We couldn't leave. There were other teams staying in the hotel, but they were living on different floors and we only saw them at a distance and in passing.

There were a couple of times during the tournament where we were scheduled to have a day off. But our staff called a practice anyway, because it was the only chance for us to go outside. When we got to the field, they told us to forget about work: we were only there for some sunshine and to get used to the heat. The Tokyo Games turned out to be the hottest Summer Olympics ever. Temperatures were routinely in the mid-thirties, with crazy-high humidity.

The day before our opening game against Japan we had a walk-through of the huge domed stadium in Sapporo. Our mood and energy shifted immediately—that's when it finally felt like we were at the Olympics.

As a female soccer player, I have to admit that I'm used to playing in front of empty stadiums. I can remember tournaments in Portugal and Cyprus where we were playing in these big stadiums with almost no fans in them. So walking into an empty stadium wasn't surprising or awkward or weird for us. And knowing that we were playing Japan in the opening game, we thought that having nobody in the stands would take away some of their home-field advantage.

There are always nerves and excitement and expectations that come with the opening match. You can't win a tournament in the first game, but you can definitely set your tournament back if you perform poorly. We knew it was going to be a close battle. Japan is always a technically gifted, organized side.

We came out flying, and I scored early in the game. (It turned out to be our only shot on net that day.) We seem to have a history of that—in the opener against Brazil in Rio, Janine Beckie scored in the first few seconds.

Then, in the second half, our keeper, Stephanie Labbé, suffered a rib injury after colliding with one of the Japanese players. The play resulted in a penalty for Japan.

The night before every game during a tournament, Steph and I always go to Mike Norris, our goalkeeper coach, and watch video of the opposing goalkeeper and potential penalty shooters. We write everything down: where they like to shoot, where their keeper tends to dive.

As Steph was getting treatment on the sidelines, we talked about who was going to take the penalty for Japan and where she liked to shoot. Though Steph had really been rocked by the collision, she was prepared. She saved the penalty and made another save on the rebound, and then had to come out of the game.

We gave up a late goal to let them tie it, and that was disappointing. But, still, we got a point against Japan, in Japan. We'd checked that box, and now it was on to the next game.

In an Olympic tournament you need to get over the highs and lows quickly, because you've got another game in two days.

Steph had been waiting her whole career for those Olympics in Japan. She was built for that moment because she'd done so much work on the mental side of the game. You might remember her smiling during those amazing shootouts in Tokyo. Steph thrived in that situation. It was incredible to watch. She was having fun. And she just owned it.

Over the years, since Steph joined the national team in 2006, we've become very close friends. Steph is just such a solid, incredible person. She knows how to have fun—she's hilarious, and never takes herself too seriously—but she also knows when it's time to get down to work.

I've seen her go through the whole journey—through struggles and peaks and injuries. Unfortunately, that seems to be the life of a goalkeeper. The rest of us have nine other players around us, so even if you're not performing at your absolute best on a given day you still feel protected. But there's only one goalkeeper. And if you're the backup, you know that the number-one keeper will be playing in 95 percent of the games. You have to wait your turn. Steph waited for years. She was the number two or number three behind Erin McLeod and Karina LeBlanc, doing the work, watching all the films, and then not playing. I can't even imagine the mental strength that must take.

It's similar for some of our field players, who get called into camp and then are cut at the end, or they make the roster but never get to see playing minutes. I have so much respect for them because I know how mad I get if I don't start a game or if I get subbed off in the eightieth minute (I know it's the right call, but still). That's who I am and how I'm wired. It takes a special kind of person to give absolutely everything day in and day out with limited opportunities to show their stuff in a match.

And that's part of what makes our national team so special. Everyone accepts her role and all the players want to help each other out. A player might not be happy about it and will push and work hard to change it, but at the end of the day, all of us are thinking about how we can help the team reach the ultimate goal.

Leading into a tournament, you look at your draw as soon as it comes out. Our coaches won't admit to such calculations out loud, but as a player, I know I count points and do the math to figure out how we get out of the group and into the next round. In the Tokyo Olympics, we needed to get a point against Japan and three points against Chile, and then we would be through, no matter what happened in our third match, which was against Great Britain.

Steph sat out the next game because of her injury. The Chile match said a lot about how women's football is evolving and growing. Chile is one of those countries that has done well in men's soccer but is just beginning to invest in the women's game. I have no doubt that we could still beat them ten times out of ten games. But we no longer win those games 10–0, given that Chile has a world-class goalkeeper and some great players.

In the first half we had chances, but we didn't score. Then Janine Beckie put one in and we all felt a sense of relief. After that we were rolling. In the second half Janine got another one, and that should have been game over. Chile hadn't created any opportunities to that point in the game. But then they got a late penalty and we started to feel some uneasiness, even though we had been dominating. Living that moment—knowing it's the Olympic Games, knowing that you really need the three points—creates a level of stress. In the end we won 2–1.

After the game, I remember Bev telling us there were things we could improve on, but with four points in the bag after two games, it was job well done. That's how you have to view things at the Olympics. If you're struggling, you can't be too hard on yourself, and if it's going great, you can't let your head get too big, because the next game comes up fast.

Getting those points against Chile did mean that a few of us could sit out the final group match against Great Britain. If you can manage to find a game where you can rest some players in a tournament, you do it. I didn't dress, Desi Scott didn't dress, and some other starters only played a few minutes. Since the national team has developed more depth within our roster, I had no doubt that we were still going to win the game.

But winning or losing didn't really mean that much in terms of who we would draw in the quarterfinals. Once you get out of your group at the Olympics, just about everyone is good, and no one knows what will happen.

As it turned out, we gave up a late own goal and the game finished 1–1.

If we had won, we would have played Australia next. With the draw, we were matched against Brazil.

Of course, though our focus was on our own games, we had been paying attention to the rest of the tournament—especially what was happening with the Americans.

Seeing Sweden destroy the United States 4–0 in their opening match was a shocker. Suddenly, we felt like the tournament was wide open. If the US team wasn't performing at its best, anyone could win.

In the months before the Olympics, the Americans hadn't played anyone notable. There was a sense that they hadn't been tested. They had some new players on the roster and a new coach who had been through the qualifying rounds but hadn't been in a tournament like the Olympics before.

My next thought was, *They're the Americans—they don't need to be tested. They always show up for the big ones.*

But as I watched them play that match, I saw some huge holes and weaknesses within their team that I don't think any of us had seen before. Sweden exploited them all.

And there was one other clue.

The Americans had played Australia immediately before our game with Great Britain, in the same stadium. The game finished in a draw.

Players who have been on the bench during a game usually run in the stadium after the game is over—especially in the Olympics. With the quick turnaround, there's not a lot of practice time between matches.

The American substitutes ran, but none of the players who had been in the game stuck around and supported them. Everyone was running in their own little section of the field.

It was something small, but it stuck in our heads. If we have players running at the end of a game, we're all out there supporting them, because they've just supported us for ninety minutes. It's the least you can do.

We felt like our tight-knit group would prove to be a difference-maker in the tournament.

The quarterfinal against Brazil was the first game we played in the Olympics with fans in the stands. Because it was in a different district of the country, the COVID rules were different, and about three thousand people came out to watch.

It feels like we always end up playing Brazil in big tournaments. And for all the talk about Brazil and "the beautiful game" and how technically gifted they are, you know it's not going to be pretty. It's going to be a scrap, an ugly one-goal game. Just as we know what they can do, they know that Canada will never back down from a fight.

It felt like nothing happened in that match for the longest time. There weren't many chances on either side. It was very tight and very close and extremely intense.

As we headed into extra time, I remember Janine turning to Jessie Fleming and saying, "This is why we always do the runs at the end of practice. We're ready for this."

Jessie ran fourteen kilometres in that game—our little Energizer Bunny. Still, by the end of extra time, everyone was just dead.

And then it came down to penalty kicks . . .

As a team, heading into a shootout, all you can do is know that you've done everything you can to be prepared. That's it. Steph and I had done our homework the day before. And the team had practised PKs from the first day in camp in Los Angeles: PKs into an open net, PKs against goalkeepers. Staff tracked every single kick we took and whether we scored or missed.

The coaches had their list of potential shooters, but still they asked each one of us individually if we wanted to take a penalty.

I was first up.

"Do you want to take one?"

"Yes."

It was so nerve-racking. Shootouts are the worst. The *worst*.

I took our first shot and I put it where I wanted. Your goal as the shooter is to force the keeper to make a great save to beat you. If they do, you're pissed, but you don't have to second-guess yourself. You didn't miss: they defended. It happens.

And it happened. The Brazil keeper made a great save.

I ripped the collar of my jersey I was so mad at myself. During the walk back to join my teammates, I was wondering, *Is this going to be the thing that costs us the chance to play for a medal?* Those are the thoughts that go through your head in a moment like that.

I stood there waiting and hoping that one of the Brazilians would miss or Steph would make a save. We were all pretty quiet. Everyone was in their own space.

But Steph said, "I'll get one. I know I'll save one."

All of our other shooters scored. And sure enough, Steph did it. She stopped Brazil's fourth shot, and then their fifth to win it.

It was nuts on the field after that final save. We all ran towards Steph, but because of the new video-assisted review (VAR) rules, we were also looking at the refs, because they had to check the video to make sure Steph hadn't left her line early. When we finally got the signal that the game was really over—oh my God, what a feeling that was.

Brazil's great star Marta (so great she's known by first name alone) was one of the first players to come give me a big hug and congratulate me. I have so much respect for Marta. I had the honour and pleasure of playing with her for a couple of years on a club team. She's one of the few players in the women's game who leaves me in awe at some of the things she can do on the field. I remember watching her beat the US all by herself at the World Cup in 2007. If she's on, Marta's unstoppable.

On the field, she's a world-beater who gets mad at opponents, gets mad at whole teams; she's so passionate about the sport and about winning. Off the field she's down to earth and fun and relaxed and plays the guitar and is a completely different person.

I admire her even more for what she's done for women's soccer globally and for young girls, especially in Brazil. She's their hope and their role model. After Brazil got knocked out of the Women's World Cup in France in 2019, she gave an amazing interview where she called on the Brazilian federation to support women's football. The passion she has is so immense. She just lives and breathes soccer every day.

After she gave me that hug, Marta looked me straight in the eye and said, "You have to beat the Americans."

I got selected for a random doping test and had to stay at the stadium for an hour after the match. By the time I got back to the hotel my teammates were eating dinner and watching the US-Holland quarterfinal on their phones. We knew we were going to play the winner.

Everyone was cheering for Holland, because everyone likes it when the underdog triumphs. But the Americans ended up winning the close match in a shootout, setting up the match we all knew was coming.

So here we go again, nine years after the highs and lows of the London Olympics.

Honestly, most times we play the US, we need to perform at our absolute best and then hope that they have a not-great day in order to have a chance to beat them. But heading into that game, the dynamic felt different. We felt different, but they did too, I think.

It was obvious that there were some holes in their team. There were some opportunities to exploit that we hadn't seen before, especially in how our midfield matched up with theirs. They seemed to rely almost entirely on individual talent, which to us made them not as dangerous as they'd been in the past.

We stayed in the same hotel as they did before the semifinal game and wondered whether they were enjoying themselves as much as we were, given all the restrictions. My teammates and I were having a blast, having *Mario Kart* tournaments and playing *Catan*.

Given the history, all the pressure was on them. For us, it was an opportunity.

We knew they were beatable. We knew that the way we played fit perfectly against them, our strength in defence countering their offence. There was no fear.

I remember looking at players who were with our team in London, like Desiree Scott and Sophie Schmidt, and thinking, *We've waited nine years for this game.* It was the same stage, in the same tournament, but we were convinced the outcome was going to be different. We were so confident.

And then the game happened.

In the first five or ten minutes, they were all over us. They were still the same old US team. All those little things that we'd thought we'd noticed didn't matter . . .

But we never felt overwhelmed. We slowly started to shift the momentum our way, handling their pressure and taking the steam out of their offensive game. They weren't creating many chances. We weren't creating many chances either, but at least we were not allowing them to play the way they wanted to play.

Steph made a couple of huge saves. And then the Americans' starting goalkeeper, Alyssa Naeher, got hurt and had to leave the game. Things seemed to be breaking our way.

I still don't know how Deanne Rose got on the end of that ball in the box. It wasn't planned that way. She's just the fastest human, and she ran it down. There was a collision with the American defender. At first, the ref awarded a goal kick to the US. But we knew that wasn't right. The ball had gone out off of an American player.

It would be decided by VAR, a relatively new tool in the game.

It felt like the review took forever. And then we got the signal: PK for us.

Jessie Fleming knew that kick was hers.

The day before the game, I had gone up to Bev and told her, plainly, that if there was a penalty to be taken, I didn't need to take it. I think people just assume I want to take them all. I don't.

"I've never seen Jessie miss," I told Bev. "If she wants to take it, let Jessie have it."

Jessie wanted it.

To be clear, we knew before the game what was supposed to happen in this situation. There was no surprise. There was no argument on the field. There was no, "I want it—no I want it."

When we came back out after the VAR, the ball was sitting in the eighteen-yard box. I grabbed it. We had been taught that it helps when a teammate is the one who gives you the ball before a penalty kick. If you allow the opponent to hand you the ball, it gives them the chance to try to get into your head. They can even drop the ball or say something to distract you. We didn't want any of that happening.

I know some people interpreted me handing Jessie the ball as a passing of the torch. Sometimes people read too much into things.

After the kick, Mike, our goalkeeper coach, came up to me. "That was class," he said.

"What do you mean?" I asked him.

"You should have seen the panic on the faces of the US staff when you picked up the ball and handed it to Jessie."

They'd assumed I was taking the PK and they had obviously done their research on me. When I passed the ball to Jessie, they didn't know what to do. Their goalkeeper had no idea where Jessie was going to shoot.

When Jessie's kick went in, I felt a huge sense of relief— even though I'd really had no doubts!

I looked at the clock and saw that we had about twenty minutes to defend the lead. And I knew we were about to face the onslaught of onslaughts, because the US team doesn't just lie down.

Here it comes.

We fought them off and fought them off, and Steph came up big again and again in goal.

Finally, the three whistles. Game over.

Oh my God, it was instant tears.

Two thoughts went through my head all at once: we had finally beaten the Americans, and we were finally going to be playing for Olympic gold.

The feeling of being on the winning side of a game like that, at last, was just indescribable. Looking back now, it almost felt like we'd won a gold medal right there, because we had knocked the Americans out.

The vets—me, Erin, Sophie, Alyssa, Steph and Desi— stayed on that field and took photos for half an hour after the match. It was incredible, knowing we were going to get a chance to play for gold, knowing what we had just done and who we had beaten. And, yeah, also enjoying a little bit of revenge.

The Americans *always* win. They're *always* number one.

I don't want to sound like I'm bashing the US team—they've done so much for women's sport by pushing standards, by pushing for equal pay with the men. They've been forerunners not only on the field but also off the field. I have so much respect for them, and I'm friends with so many of them.

But, man, when you put on your national team jersey, you want to win.

It was fun going back to the hotel that night, with the shoe finally on the other foot. It felt *so* nice.

And then it was time to win a gold medal.

2

"MAKE SURE YOU COME BACK ALIVE"

I grew up in South Burnaby, British Columbia—born and raised on the Lower Mainland. My whole family is from around there.

I didn't really know my dad's side of the family. He was estranged from them. My brother, Michael, and I knew his mom a little bit, but when it came to family, everything else was my mom's side—the Gants. She was one of six kids, and her whole family lived near us. The Gants are a big, old-fashioned, cheesy family like the kind you used to see on TV.

Everyone went to my maternal grandparents' house at least once a week, and their door was always open to us. Besides my parents, my grandparents were the most important people in my life until they passed away. You hear people talk about the matriarch and patriarch of a family? That was them.

It didn't have to be a formal visit. It was more like, "Hey, do you want to go to Grandma and Grandpa's house?" And we'd just go.

And Christmas? Oh my God. They still lived in the teeny house in Burnaby where they'd raised their six kids. On Christmas Day they would cook dinner for everyone, and somehow we fit thirty or forty people into that little house.

My grandparents are gone now. Yet the only time in my life we've missed having a big family Christmas dinner was in December 2020, the first pandemic holiday season. The next year we all got together at my aunt and uncle's house. Michael and I cooked the turkey, and no one died after eating it, so that was a success. It was just the way Christmas should be.

Growing up, I was very close with my cousins. One aunt and uncle lived just down the street from us, and they had a pool where we hung out. As a kid, I preferred spending time with Michael and my cousins or going to my grandparents' house over hanging around with any of my friends. That's just how I was. That's how I still am.

Things were different for kids back then. Our parents both worked—my mom at the Royal Bank and my dad in construction. We did not have a ton of money, but my parents made it work, paycheque to paycheque. My brother and I got ourselves to school and got ourselves home from school. Then we would head for the park on our own, which kids nowadays probably aren't allowed to do. It felt like we were outside all the time. We were definitely not the type who wanted to sit inside and read. I have nothing against reading; we just preferred being active.

I can't believe the freedom we had. We had a key to the house and the only real rule was "Make sure you come back alive."

Any time he could, my dad loved to be out playing with us; he was a big kid at heart. Mom was always the serious one.

Pretty much everything we did included sports. We'd go to Christmas dinner and bring along a change of clothes because we knew we'd end up at the park. Or we'd play hockey in the back alley. If the weather was bad, we'd play some kind of game in the hall, especially Michael and me.

Now kids are on their iPads and phones all the time. Obviously, we didn't have that, but we had an unfinished basement in our house, and we took full advantage. Hockey, soccer . . . we would rollerblade down there. We played football down there. We destroyed it. The number of windows and light fixtures that were broken—well, that's what we did with our free time. Even as we got older, Michael and I would still be out playing in the yard. I don't think we ever grew out of that. To this day when we're around each other, one of us will say, "Ping-Pong?" Game on.

Michael is three years older than me. When we were kids, we had the typical love/hate sibling relationship. My mom liked to talk about the times she grounded both of us because of something we had done, and we'd be so livid with each other—yeah, it wasn't pretty. There were multiple incidents with hockey sticks being swung like baseball bats and things like that.

She'd send us to our rooms, which were right beside each other on the second level of the house. But we figured out that I could climb out my window and into his. My parents would lock us away in our separate rooms and then, two hours later, they'd find us both in Michael's room playing video games. "What the heck? Now you're friends?"

As adults, Michael and I are super close. He has a wife and two kids, my nieces, and they're just little spitfires. Being an aunt is the best. I've never wanted kids of my own, so hanging out with them and yet being able to hand them back, spoiling them rotten and then being able to say, "Here, you can deal with the sugar high"—that's great.

When it came to sports, my brother and I were carrying on a family tradition. Everyone was into sports. My mom ran track in high school: I remember seeing a newspaper article about her from back then. Her two brothers, Brian and Bruce Gant, both played pro for the Portland Timbers in the old North American Soccer League (NASL). There's a sweet black-and-white picture of Bruce playing against Johan Cruyff, the incredible Dutch footballer who won the Ballon d'Or three times in the 1970s—we've got that one framed.

Naturally, I got signed up for soccer, like everyone else in the family. I also played baseball, basketball and volleyball, and ran track and cross-country.

But soccer was the big one because it was part of our family culture. My dad coached and managed the Vancouver Firefighters team in the men's premier league in BC. I grew up on the sidelines of soccer games and fell in love with the sport. My brother and I would go to their practices on weekends and after school and shag balls for them. We loved it.

I also grew up watching my brother's games. Dad coached Michael's teams starting from the U5 level (for kids five years of age and younger) and continuing all the way through youth soccer. He'd also let me practise with them. I think Michael was okay with his little sister being there all the time, and I could definitely keep up. But given the chance he would flatten me in a tackle. I think it helped toughen me up.

My first team was called the Burnaby Bees. There wasn't a U5 team then, but I wanted to play so badly that my parents signed me up with a U7 team. I was only four. I don't remember any of this, but I've been told I was so overwhelmed that I spent lots of games on the sideline, crying.

I guess it didn't traumatize me too much. I'm still playing.

The following year, the South Burnaby Men's Club (now the South Burnaby Metro Club) formed a U6 team, and I joined that. I ended up playing with a lot of those same kids throughout my run playing youth soccer. We destroyed everything in our path: we went something like five years without losing a game. My mom coached my soccer team. If you'd had the chance to ask her, she would have told you that she taught me everything. She was very involved in youth sports in Burnaby and was voted the first female president of the South Burnaby Metro Club.

I also played T-ball with the same group of girls. We all became friends and our families became friends and one sports season led into the next sports season. Where I grew up, you can play outside all year long so long as you don't mind a little rain and a little gravel (yes, we trained on gravel).

Outside of sports, I was a shy kid. Super shy. Awkwardly shy. I hung out with a close little group of friends at school, and we were always the active ones. There would be three of us girls playing tag with four or five boys.

I was always good in school. I'm a little bit of a perfectionist with everything I do. Maybe even kind of a nerd when it came to my schoolwork. I didn't really do too much wrong or get in trouble. I wasn't there to stir things up unless it involved my brother: I'd always do whatever I could to get him in trouble. Once, I caught him leaving the school grounds when he shouldn't have, and I tattled on him. He ended up with a week-long suspension.

Yeah, Michael, that was me.

I was a natural at sports, but I also definitely worked at it, even though it didn't feel like work. It was what I wanted to do.

We had a cement wall in our front yard, and I would spend hours upon hours launching lacrosse balls off it and fielding them. My brother and I played all sorts of sports together, or with a couple of the neighbours. In hockey, I was always in goal. I played baseball just as much as I played soccer, and, honestly, I maybe even liked baseball more. I was absolutely convinced I was going to play for the Toronto Blue Jays. I was always a Blue Jays' fan. They were my team before and after they won back-to-back World Series in the 1990s. Robbie Alomar was who I wanted to be. Back then, all I knew was that he was the greatest second baseman of all time. I played second base and I wore number 12 because of him. And I really thought that I was going to take his position when he was done.

I still wear number 12.

Unfortunately, I didn't have any female athletes I looked up to when I was a kid. It wasn't until I was thirteen or fourteen that I became aware of the American soccer player Michelle Akers and her stellar performance in the first Women's World Cup in 1991—and in Canada, Andrea Neil and Charmaine Hooper. But when I was little, there were no obvious role models and no obvious career paths in women's sports. I'm sure that's why I was convinced I was going to be on the Jays. At least you could see them on television.

Soccer was just something I loved. It was my freedom. No stress. Just playing a game. I never imagined it could be my life.

But I think, from a young age, there was an understanding that I was good. There were times when my team won 8–0 and I scored six of the goals. My soccer-playing uncles would talk about how they could tell I saw the game differently than the other kids did. Everyone else was in a clump chasing around and I would be standing in position waiting for the ball to come out.

My parents never pressured me in any way. They always wanted what was best for me and for me to be happy. I remember sitting in the car with my dad when he drove me to my first tryout for a regional team. If I made it, I would be playing in a tournament in front of the provincial head coach.

I will never forget my dad saying, "Are you sure you want to do this? None of your friends are going to be here. You don't know any of these people. Are you sure this is what you want to do?"

And I said, "Yeah, let's do it."

My family shaped who I am. They didn't get too caught up in anything. They would never let my head get too big or let me get too down. They always reminded me that, ultimately, it was just a game.

I made the team that day—I was eleven and it was a U14 side.

That team gave me my first experience of travelling to play. We went down to Los Angeles and played in tournaments in San Francisco. That was also the first time I was exposed to US soccer. Suddenly there were university coaches watching us. I realized that maybe my soccer world could be bigger than just my little club team in Burnaby.

The coach of that provincial team was Keith Puiu. He took a chance on a little kid, the same way Even Pellerud later took a chance on me when he selected me to play for Canada. I owe them both a lot.

Our season ran from late spring through summer. At the end of it, Keith had individual meetings with all the players, and I remember him saying to me, "Look, if you keep up with what you're doing, you'll be on the national team as a teenager."

Who? What? Me?

I had just turned twelve.

I started to become aware of people with clipboards standing on the sidelines at my games, scouting for US colleges. When you're that young they can't approach you directly, but it was hard not to notice them.

I skipped a year in local youth soccer when I went into eighth grade, which meant I stopped playing with all my best friends and started playing with players who were on the provincial team with me. They were older than I was and looking for opportunities for scholarships. That's when I started taking the game a little more seriously and thinking that I wanted that, too.

I didn't mind the pressure, because in a way I didn't understand it. Soccer still wasn't make-it-or-break-it for me, even knowing that there were university coaches at my games. I was still a kid and I was still having fun.

I'm competitive by nature, but I don't think I'm over-competitive. I hate to lose, but that's not what really fuels my fire. I'm more the type who is motivated by wanting to get better. I don't spend every minute thinking about how I'm going to beat you. Maybe that's a flaw in me, but it's never been what drives me. It's always been more about the internal challenge.

I first noticed something was up with my mother's health when I was seven or eight. She was a little bit more rigid, and a little slower, and she walked with an uneven gait.

By the time I was twelve or thirteen, she had started to use a cane. That's when my parents sat my brother and me down and explained to us that Mom had multiple sclerosis.

I had no idea what MS was. There wasn't any internet then. Nowadays, you can just google it. Our parents tried their best to explain it to us. But I don't think even they really understood what was coming.

As I said, my mom was an athlete, as active as the rest of us. And now we were seeing that taken away from her by a disease.

Later, I found out that my mother had been diagnosed with MS when she was pregnant with my brother. She ended up living with it for more than forty years.

When you're a kid, you think that your parents are unbreakable. But my brother and I learned, at an age when we couldn't really process it, how fragile life is, and that our parents weren't going to live forever.

I remember being embarrassed about my mom's condition, which is so messed up. I didn't want people to see that she was sick. And I know she was embarrassed too. She didn't want people to know. Our family is very good at putting on a brave front, and that's what we tried to do, which I know maybe doesn't make sense.

I was so thankful for my extended family. My mom's brothers and sister and my grandparents became a team. And I remember my dad trying to be the caregiver. It was hard. It was very hard. After I moved away for college and my brother got married and moved out, it was a lot for my dad to deal with on his own.

Becoming comfortable talking to people about my mom and MS was a slow process. I had one teammate in youth soccer whose mom also had MS, and it was nice to know that at least I wasn't alone, that other people were dealing with it as well. And then in college two of my teammates had parents with MS. I think that really helped me become more open about it. There was a little group of us who could share stories and cry together.

My mom was stubborn and sarcastic (I got that from her). And she was the strongest person I have ever known. She went through so much because of MS—many surgeries and many stays in the ICU. More than once, someone in the family came up to me and said, "We don't understand how your mom is still alive." I didn't have an answer other than that she was a fighter, and that she lived for the moment. She lived for her grandkids, for tournaments of mine, for the weekends when my brother and his wife and the kids could visit.

But it was so hard for her. I don't want to paint too rosy a picture of her life. I would've given up. I've told my family—if I ever get to that point, please just pull the plug. But my mom was a fighter. She continued to give me crap right up until the end of her life—she died in the spring of 2022—and that was perfect.

3

YOU AIM HIGH, RIGHT?

The 1999 World Cup, hosted by the United States, was the event that changed women's soccer—especially if you were a member of the American team.

One of the tournament groups was based in Portland, and our coaches took us down there for a weekend to see a couple of games. The World Cup games in Portland weren't like the scenes many of us remember of the American team winning the gold in a shootout in front of ninety thousand fans in the Rose Bowl, the Brandi Chastain moment where she whipped off her jersey and whirled it around her head and ran around in her sports bra and all the rest. The matches were in the old Civic Stadium, and there were people in the stands—a lot of people. Not the hundred fans we might see for one of our bigger games, but ten thousand people. As the tournament progressed, those crowds grew to as many as twenty thousand. I remember realizing for the first time that there were women playing soccer for a living. By the end of the 1999 World Cup, the stars of the US team had become more famous than just about any female athletes in the history of the world.

It's nuts, thinking back, that I would end up playing in the next World Cup after that one.

That 1999 tournament wasn't such a great moment for the Canadian women's national team. They drew their first group match 1–1 against Japan, and then lost their next two, 7–1 to Norway and 4–1 to Russia. After they were knocked out, the Canadian Soccer Association replaced the coach, Neil Turnbull, with a Norwegian, Even Pellerud, who had won the 1995 World Cup coaching Norway's women's team, along with a bronze medal at the 1996 Olympics.

One of the first things Even did after taking the job was travel across Canada scouting players.

I was sixteen, but I was playing periodically on a women's team along with Andrea Neil and Silvana Burtini, who were both already on the national team. There was an all-star game on the Lower Mainland that was staged just so that Even could get a look at some players. I was one of them.

I don't think I really understood the significance. I was so young. And joining the national team seemed so out of reach—not because of what I was or wasn't doing on the field, but because I was just a kid.

After that game Even held a camp in BC to which he invited forty players from across Canada. He asked me to be a part of it. I remember thinking: "What?!"

Sometimes you're just in the right place at the right time. My ability would have gotten me to the national team at some point, but having a new coach, in a new World Cup cycle, who brought in a bunch of young players, sped things up. Even had watched the Canadian team in the 1999 World Cup and he knew that a similar roster was not going to be successful. He realized he had to start almost from scratch.

I remember being so intimidated by him. Everyone was saying that he was going to be so hard on us. He *was* different from the coaches I was used to, but I always got along well with him. He took me under his wing, and at times, sending me out to play against the best in the world, it also felt like he was feeding me to the wolves—I guess for my own good.

But Even also definitely protected me, as I think he protected a lot of the younger players. He knew that at some point we would be the future of this team. I credit him with so much. I have so much respect for him.

I know a lot of people weren't fans of his style of play. It was very direct, with lots of long balls, similar to the way they used to play in England. But with the team that we had, with the players that we had, it was effective.

Eventually, the team progressed to the point where we needed to move on and play a more modern, possession- and passing-oriented style, but I credit him with being the one who changed the program. He was the first coach to fight the CSA for budget, and camps, and games, and tournaments. He went and sought out Greg Kerfoot, who owned the Vancouver Whitecaps soccer team, for help. He got team residencies funded, where we'd gather for weeks of meetings and practise. I credit him for starting all of that. He single-handedly forced the CSA to pay attention to the women's team.

Charmaine Hooper was on the national team for twenty years, and she finished her career with 129 caps. (Soccer players are "capped" every time they play internationally for their country.) That tells you how few matches they were playing. By the time I was twenty the game had grown so much that I had already played one hundred games for Canada. That was because of Even and his fight for the program and for opportunities.

It wasn't always pretty at the beginning. We lost some games 9–0. But you've got to start somewhere.

Even could sometimes be harsh. After we lost badly to Brazil in the Pan Am Games, he made the whole team sit and watch the match film. We were all together in a room for what had to be four hours while he stopped and started the footage, pointing out every single mistake that anyone had made.

He was also a fitness freak. I remember once when we were in the US and about to play the Americans, he made me run the hotel stairs with my teammate Randee Hermus on my back. Why that would ever be necessary I'm not sure, but I remember Even saying that if we wanted to compete with the Americans we had to be at least as fit as them. He was the coach who started that push for player athleticism and fitness.

I didn't always agree with Even's methods. He sent us off for recovery runs around Burnaby Lake—that's a ten-kilometre distance, which is not a recovery run.

But he could also be nice. And he was kind of a goofball. We used to train out at the old University of British Columbia field. He lived on the North Shore, and I'll never forget him pulling up for our practices on a scooter in his little helmet. *Who is this man?*

Before the Olympics in Beijing in 2008, Even gave us a project to do. Quote/unquote—a "project." He'd decided that everyone had to do a presentation on themselves so we could truly get to know each other. We had people playing guitar. We had people doing inappropriate dancing. I just told my story. I don't have any hidden talents and am not about to bust out a guitar, or anything else for that matter.

So, yes, he had some different methods. But God, he got us some results. He moved the program forward. Every time I see him now, we have a giant hug. I know that he probably wasn't everyone's favourite. But I owe him so much in my career.

But I'm getting ahead of myself.

As I said, Even brought quite a few young players into the team. It wasn't just me, and I think that helped me feel comfortable. Randee, the teammate I carried up the stairs, was also from BC, and joined the team at the same time I did. We kind of stuck together and were roommates for a long time.

There were also some veteran players I became close with: Andrea Neil, Silvana Burtini and Nicci Wright. I had been playing and training with them in BC for a good year before I joined the national team. They were all big personalities and they took care of me. But I also think they could tell that I could play soccer. So that helped . . .

Charmaine Hooper—two-time NCAA (National Collegiate Athletic Association) first-team All-American in her university career, who had just been a crucial part of the national team's first-ever CONCACAF (Confederation of North, Central America, and Caribbean Association Football) gold in 1998—scared me. Not because of anything she did or said, but because she's Charmaine and she's intimidating; she speaks her mind and she doesn't hold back. But I learned so much from her. I learned how to work. I learned how to train. I was always taught that if you want to be the best, you watch what the best person on the team is doing and you copy them. I remember watching Charmaine running hills and sprints at the end of practice and thinking that people don't get to the top by a fluke. They work for it.

My first tournament playing for Canada was the 2000 Algarve Cup in Portugal. That was also the first time in my life that I had flown overseas, and the first time I encountered the stars of the US World Cup–winning team in person. I got into an elevator with Mia Hamm and Michelle Akers and thought, *Just make sure you don't pee yourself.*

Our opening game was against China. That was also overwhelming, because I had just watched them on TV in the World Cup final against the US. It was also Even's first game as coach. His instructions to me were, "You're playing 90 minutes. Go."

What? I don't understand. This can't be happening . . .

We lost to China.

Our second game was against Norway, another power-house, as well as Even's old team. I scored my first goal for Canada. It was just crazy.

Our final match was against Denmark. We won 3–2 and I scored two more goals.

I remember sitting in my hotel room in Portugal thinking about how many goals Mia Hamm had scored so far in her career. I wasn't necessarily setting my eyes on that number, just thinking, *Wow, that's a lot of goals.* But I *was* kind of setting my eyes on that number, and then when Abby Wambach surpassed Mia's record, I started thinking about how many she was scoring.

As my career went on, I kept track. *Okay, this is how many goals I've scored in so many games. Mia had this number of goals in so many games. So okay, I'm on pace.* When Abby beat Mia's record, I used her as my internal yardstick. I'd be lying if I said breaking the record never crossed my mind.

I didn't necessarily think I could do it. I knew it would take a lot of luck and longevity. But yeah, I had my eye on it, almost from the beginning.

You aim high, right?

4

YES, I HAD A
SOCCER-BALL FLIP PHONE

I never know quite how to just come out with something like this—with all the family programming I received about never sounding big-headed—but I think I got athletic scholarship offers from everywhere. Each day there'd be stuff in the mailbox from different schools all over the United States.

I eventually narrowed it down to my top four: the University of Portland (UP), the University of North Carolina, the University of Connecticut (UConn), and the University of Nebraska—the latter because they had a Canadian head coach, John Walker. Also, at that time, all kinds of Canadian players went there: Amy Walsh, Karina LeBlanc, Sharolta Nonen, and then later Brittany Timko.

My choices were, literally, all over the map.

I also considered the University of British Columbia, much closer to home. My dad and I went out there and met with the coach, Dick Mosher. If I had decided to go there, it would have been for the academics. Mosher was very honest about not being able to compete with what the US schools had to offer when it came to financial support.

I knew a lot more about the Pacific Northwest than I did about Nebraska or North Carolina or Connecticut. I had been down to Portland a little bit when I was growing up. I never saw my uncles play for the Timbers—that was before my time—but Uncle Brian stayed on there after his career ended. Pretty much every summer we'd go down as a family and visit him. We would also go to the beach along the Oregon coast, where we were the only weird ones who swam in the freezing cold Pacific Ocean. ("Oh, they must be Canadians . . .") Over the years I had also been to Oregon for tournaments with the BC provincial team and for Nike camps.

Around the time I was making my decision, the national team held a camp in Nebraska, so I had a chance to go there for the first time and see the school. Nothing against the University of Nebraska, but as soon as I landed, I realized I was a West Coaster, and this was definitely not the West Coast. There was no water. There was nothing. Lincoln, Nebraska, is also such a college football town. Every conversation seemed to start with, "Oh, but our football team . . ." That would be great if I played football, but I didn't. The vibe of the town just wasn't for me.

So, then it was down to the other three. Well, actually, UConn was kind of the spare. My choice was between Portland and North Carolina.

Both coaches travelled to Burnaby on official recruiting visits, where they come to your house, meet the family and try to persuade you that their school and their program is the right fit for you.

Anson Dorrance, who is still the head coach of North Carolina, drove up to the house in a sports car—the fanciest car I had ever seen in my life. He brought books—about *him*—that had sticky notes on pages that he wanted me and my family to read. I'll never forget him handing out those books. I thought it was kind of cool until he handed one to my brother and my brother handed it right back to him. "You're not recruiting me," he said. (I was so embarrassed.)

My parents made dinner for Anson, and I guess the visit went okay. But it didn't seem like he usually had to do much to recruit players because they came to him. That was the sense we all got. But it was also true at the time, and it's still true to this day—if you're good and they'll take you, you go to North Carolina because it is an incredibly successful program.

Anson also wouldn't guarantee me a full-ride scholarship for my freshman year, which was a joke given what my family could actually afford. My parents told me, "Look, if this is where you want to go, we will find a way to make it work." But I knew it would be a huge financial strain on them.

Then Clive Charles, the coach from the University of Portland, came up for his visit. He already had a strong connection to my family. His wife is Canadian, and they had a place in North Burnaby that my parents rented after Clive moved down to Portland to play with the Timbers. My brother spent the first six months of his life in that apartment, though they'd moved before I was born.

Clive had played with my uncles, and became a friend of the family, including my grandparents. Everyone knew Clive. I remember when each of my grandparents passed away, we went through old photo albums to put together a slide show for their funerals and there were all kinds of pictures of Clive. But even though he was a family friend, I didn't know him well at all before that visit.

First, Clive took me and my family out to dinner in a restaurant. We talked about my soccer for maybe five minutes. He was more interested in what I wanted to do with my life after soccer. He had big hopes for me as a player, he said, but you never know how things are going to pan out.

He was interested in what kind of person I was, and what kind of a student I was. "Do you think you'd flourish in a big class? Small class? Do you know what you want to study? Do you know what you want to be?" He asked questions that mattered. It didn't feel like I was just a commodity to him.

It was a stark contrast to how Anson operated.

Clive had a good program—not as good as North Carolina's, where it seemed they were always challenging for a national title, but Portland was a perennial top six or eight team in the country. Clive coached both the women's and men's teams, which was pretty unique. And, he said, "I think I can help you as a soccer player."

After dinner we went to my grandparents' house and hung out, and a couple of my uncles came over. At that point it didn't feel like a recruiting visit anymore.

Not long after that, I went down to Portland with my family to visit Uncle Brian, but also to go see the university. It wasn't an official trip or anything like that, just a chance to have a look around. We watched one of their home games and it was something I had never experienced— a university team playing in front of three thousand fans. It was nuts.

After that weekend we went home to Burnaby. I remember coming down for family dinner the next day and announcing, "Guys, I'm going to call Clive and tell him I want to go to Portland."

Right away I called him at home, using my soccer-ball phone—because I was so cheesy that I had the little flip phone that looked like a soccer ball. When he answered, I could tell he was having dinner himself. He said, "That is amazing, but can we talk tomorrow?"

So that's how I committed to the University of Portland.

And then I called Anson Dorrance to let him know that I wasn't going to be playing for North Carolina.

"Are you sure?" he said. "We just found a full-ride scholarship for you for your freshman year."

"Yes, I'm sure," I said. "I'll see you next year." Meaning when we played against his team.

I was still finishing up my last year in high school. If you make an early commitment to an NCAA program, you can still change your mind, renege, and commit to a different school, so long as you do it within a certain amount of time.

North Carolina won the national championship that year. The day after, Anson called me again.

"Are you sure you still want to go to the University of Portland?"

"Yes," I told him. "One hundred percent."

Clive built the sport of soccer in the city of Portland. I play now for the Thorns at Providence Park, and it's cool to walk out every day and see Clive's name and his number, which was retired by the Timbers. Inside the stadium they have a black-and-white photo of Clive and my uncle Brian back in their NASL playing days. That's pretty neat.

When I got there, the University of Portland team was the perennial runner-up, losing in the semifinals, or losing in the final. The team had never won a national championship. It's a small school, and it didn't really have much to attract athletes other than soccer players and cross-country runners. If you were a person looking for a football school, Portland wasn't the place. There is a basketball program, but it's not like you're coming to Duke. UP was soccer to the core. Clive created something unique there. We always liked to say that the true soccer players chose Portland.

Playing university soccer at Portland had a big impact on me as an athlete. By this point, I was already on Canada's national team, but that commitment was two weeks here, a week there. You're not living and breathing that level of soccer all the time. In Burnaby, the club soccer was decent, but it's not the same. Suddenly, in Portland, the soccer was—wow—and I was in that environment day in and day out.

I was talented coming in as a freshman. I knew how to play. But learning how to train and compete at that level was an adjustment for me. Not that it was super hard, but it was just eye-opening. It wasn't a job, but it was *like* a job. When you're being paid with a scholarship to perform, it's such an uptick in level. Also, the US talent pool is unbelievable. The players on the university squad were not all going to make national teams, but everyone was so skilled, so technically sound. I wasn't used to that.

At the same time, there's a reason why not all of those college players go on to play pro. It's because soccer isn't necessarily their ultimate passion in life. That's the big difference in playing for a national team versus college soccer—the level of passion. It's win at all costs on the national team. Everyone is willing to do anything to fight for the country on their jersey.

There were a few other Canadians in the Portland program. Wanda Rozwadowska was on the team. Elsa Hume was there for my senior year. And Sophie Schmidt came in after I was gone. Clive always joked that he needed at least one Canadian on his roster, and that anything more than two was too many. Though he did relish his Canadian connections. Whenever my parents would come down to see us play, Clive and Bill Irwin, who was our goalkeeper coach (like Clive, he was from the UK but had spent time in Canada), would get them to bring ketchup chips and HP Sauce. In those days you couldn't buy either in Portland. My parents would be smuggling snacks across the border for my coaches.

Clive was genuine and caring and kind. Just a good guy. At the same time, he commanded respect without having to do or say anything, just by being the ultimate professional. And he was a jokester. He had a way of taking stress off players.

I don't know if this exactly falls within NCAA rules, but I remember him making a bet with one of my teammates at practice one day.

"I bet I can race you to the half line."

"Clive," the player said, "there's no way you're going to beat me. What are we betting?"

Money.

She took off and Clive just walked to the half line.

"I never said I was going to beat you," he said. "I just said I could race you. Pay up."

And he was serious.

The school itself was a perfect fit for me. The university has just over three thousand undergrads, which was fewer people than in my high school in Burnaby. Instead of being in a class of eight hundred in freshman year, I was in a class of twenty-five. I studied biology—I didn't make it easy on myself—but the professors were there to help and work with you. Because it was a smaller school, they were able to.

I wanted to be a physical therapist. That was always plan A—until it became plan B. My high school had a grade-twelve work experience program, and I went and worked at the 8 Rinks recreational facility in Burnaby in the physical therapy area. It was great. That was always what I wanted to be, but I think I'm done with school. I have a lot of teammates who have managed to take classes while playing and I just don't know how they do that. One former teammate of mine, Nadia Nadim, became a doctor while playing soccer. An actual medical doctor, working in the hospital. How do you have time for that?

I did graduate from university, and I was a good student—an Academic All-American. It wasn't a cakewalk. UP wasn't like some of those big sports schools in the United States where people do homework for their athletes. It was almost the opposite, a place where an education came first, and soccer came second.

One year I needed a couple of extra credits, and I was already carrying a pretty heavy academic load. Now I admit I'm not an artsy type, but I signed up for a ballet class along with a bunch of other athletes. You can imagine what a sight that class was. Nothing like waking up first thing in the morning and going to ballet.

—

Still, when I went away to school, I was torn about not being there for my mother or father. But one of the reasons I chose to attend UP was that it was relatively close to home. It allowed me to go back to Burnaby as much as possible, and it allowed my parents to come down for our home games.

And then one day during my freshman year, I got a phone call. It's weird—I can't even remember who it was from now. I think probably one of my aunts. Whoever it was, she told me that Mom had been in a car accident and was at Burnaby General.

It happened on Fraser Street in Vancouver. Mom was headed straight through the intersection on a green light. Another car, coming from the opposite direction, turned left in front of her. It didn't end well.

In the moment, I didn't understand the implications. I think my family tried to ease me into it. My mom had broken her femur, and her opposite ankle was shattered, but that didn't seem like a matter of life or death. I thought she would heal from it and, maybe a year later, she'd be fine.

But because of her MS, she wasn't ever going to be fine.

As soon as I could I went up to visit her. I had never seen her in hospital before, so that was a shock.

Before the accident she walked with a hitch in her step and used a cane. But she was still working, still driving. She never did any of that again after the accident.

That summer, when I came home after my first year, she was doing physiotherapy many times a week. But you could just tell that she wasn't going to walk again. The accident had caused so much damage, and someone with MS wasn't ever going to be able to regain their full strength. She was in a wheelchair for the rest of her life.

The accident changed my parents' lives completely. I remember them building a ramp so Mom could get in and out of the house. They had to retrofit the interior for wheelchair access. I don't know how Dad did it. It took a toll on him. Thank God, our extended family chipped in the best they could, but mainly my mom and dad just tried to deal with everything themselves. Eventually it got to the point where we said, *Mom, you need help—Dad needs help*. But at the beginning they managed alone.

It was hard to go back to school, knowing my mom was struggling and my dad was struggling, and here I was living a dream. My time at UP was amazing. UP was perfect for me. On the one hand, I was having the time of my life playing soccer in an amazing program, eventually winning national championships, getting a degree, meeting new people.

But the other side of my life was what was going on back in Burnaby.

After the accident, my parents still came down to Portland for every one of my home games, my mom in her wheelchair. It became their new normal, and I guess they made the best of it. Once you've realized that that's where you're at and this is what your life is going to be like, you make a choice.

My mom chose to live.

In the past few years, with her permission, I've started sharing my mom's story and have publicly joined the fight against MS. It's an awful disease. It affects not just the person with the disease, but their entire family. And it isn't that well-known, even though it's prevalent in Canada. I want to increase awareness, hopefully raise some money, and try to put an end to it, though I know that's not going to happen any time soon. And now I do it in my mother's memory.

5

MY BEST MOMENT ON A SOCCER FIELD

In 2002, the summer after my mom's car accident, I was selected to the Canadian team for the Under-19 Women's World Championship, the first time FIFA (the Fédération Internationale de Football Association) had ever staged a women's world youth tournament. Canada was the host country, and games were going to be played in Victoria, Vancouver and Edmonton.

Oh my God, that was a whirlwind. So unexpected. A few of us had already been called up to play for the senior national team—me, Erin McLeod, Brit Timko. But we really had no idea what we were getting ourselves into with the U19 tournament. I don't think Canada knew. I don't think the Canadian Soccer Association knew.

The U19 team prepared for the tournament for a year. Erin and I hadn't been with them the whole time, because we had been with Even and the senior team. But our teammates had had more preparation than any Canadian youth team had had before or has since. Nowadays, our youth teams will go to a qualifying tournament without even having a camp. So how do you expect them to be successful? That's why, when the CSA says to someone like me, "Can't you see that things have progressed and things are better," my answer is, "Actually, no."

Heading in, we had calculated how many games we were going to play through to the final, and we decided that we were going to go on a twelve-game win streak—at least, that was the kids' version of what was going to happen.

I remember showing up at Commonwealth Stadium for our first game against Denmark and thinking, *What are all these people doing here? Is there a game going on that I don't know about?* Here were twenty-five thousand Canadians who came out to watch a bunch of teenagers play soccer. *Female* teenagers. Nothing like that had ever happened in Canada.

We won 3–2, and our momentum just built, and built, and built through the tournament. Our team was so good. Sometimes Canadian sides have had to claw their way through tournaments. We steamrolled our way through that one. With every passing game, we just got better, the number of fans grew . . . and Erin's hairstyles got worse. Just saying.

We beat Japan 4–0 and Nigeria 2–0 to finish the group stage undefeated.

My brother and my aunt flew in for the quarterfinals. I remember them saying, "We'll just come for this one game. We have to go back to work."

In the quarterfinals, we beat England 6–2 and I scored five times. I don't know if I've scored five goals in one match since. England wasn't a bad team at all. But every so often in sports everything goes right. Everything I touched in that game found the back of the net. I remember on one of the goals, a teammate was on a breakaway and she hit the post. The ball bounced right to me and I tapped it in.

You don't win many quarterfinals in World Cups or world championships with that kind of score line. That game cemented for us that we had a legit chance to win it all—and it also created a lot of buzz around Edmonton.

Afterwards, my brother and my aunt decided they had to fly back for the semifinal. They ended up making the trip to Edmonton four times. I told them, "You could have just stayed."

This was in a time before social media. But we'd watch the television news and it was on. Or we'd see newspapers and the tournament was on the front page. I remember taking pictures of signs at the venue saying "Sold Out." Which gave us a sense of the excitement in Edmonton even if we didn't fully understand that it was happening across the country. It turned out to be a lot of excitement!

It was an amazing feeling to be at the centre of that, especially when you're so young and often don't feel the weight of expectations the way you do when you get older.

Of course, we wanted to win. And, of course, we were under some pressure because it was a world championship. But we were surrounded by our friends and we were still having fun. We did things like a team-bonding trip to play laser tag. And I had the idea that we should do a thing my dad had done with teams he coached—a Bad Kit Day. The idea was that the players would show up for practice wearing the worst-looking soccer kit that they could come up with.

Before the tournament started, I had told everyone to bring something along to Edmonton for Bad Kit Day. Apparently, there was some misunderstanding. I showed up in my Mia Hamm jersey with American socks and shorts and everything—which was the kind of bad kit I was talking about. But one of our players came dressed as a pony. Someone else wore their figure-skating outfit. And we still had to practise, which, somehow, we did. Just a bunch of kids, living their dream, playing at home in a World Championship.

The semifinal was against Brazil in front of more than thirty-seven thousand fans.

That tournament was the first time Marta and I played against each other. She was sixteen and, whoa, she was good. She's one of the few players who can just put a game on her shoulders, put her whole team on her shoulders and decide, "I'm going to score." I'm the type of player who needs their teammates. I'll put the ball in the back of the net if everything goes right. But I'm not one who's going to dribble through everyone on the other team— and man, she could do that. She's so impressive.

It was such an even game. Since that tournament, every time we play Brazil it's never pretty. They like to scrap. That's how they thrive and that's how they have been very successful over the years. I'm pretty sure we've had more red cards in games against Brazil than any other team we've played.

Clare Rustad put us ahead with a goal in injury time at the end of the first half, and then Marta scored to tie it in the sixty-ninth minute. It was a rough game. Kara Lang wound up with a terrible bloody nose, and Carmelina Moscato hurt her foot and was taken off on a stretcher.

Then, in added time, I got knocked down in the box, and we were awarded a penalty. It got ugly at that point. The Brazil coach argued the call, and when he wouldn't leave the field, the referee ejected him.

Taking a penalty is such a mind game. I wish that I had the self-confidence of Cristiano Ronaldo. It doesn't matter if he's missed three in a row; his attitude is still *Give it to me, I'm going to score.* He just oozes belief. That's never been me. I've experienced the highest of highs taking penalties and making big ones, and I've experienced the lowest of lows, missing big ones and thinking you've cost your team a game.

If I made that penalty, it would be a "golden goal." We'd win and we would be into the final.

But the keeper—Giselle—saved it, and we played on.

There was a bit of a scrum with the Brazilian players after my shot, and I think Marta kind of celebrated the miss, but I honestly don't remember that much about it. I focused on what we had to do to win the game.

In the end it went to PKs. Talk about nerves. We all have PTSD from shootouts. That's the truth.

But to experience a shootout at that age, in that environment, in front of a crowd like that was a whole other thing. We had entered that tournament with the goal of winning it all, and then it all came down to penalties, which isn't so different from a coin toss.

Marta started it off for Brazil, and Erin made an amazing save to stop her. Advantage Canada.

Candace Chapman was up first for us, and her shot was saved by the Brazil keeper, who had obviously come off her line before it was taken, but that wasn't called.

Brazil's next shooter hit the post. Advantage Canada, again.

It was my turn next.

There's no worse feeling than missing a penalty during the game and then walking out to take one in the shootout. It was maybe the only penalty I've ever taken where I didn't know where I was going to shoot as I was running up to the ball. I was flying blind on that one. But as I approached the ball, I glanced at the keeper, because some keepers have a tendency to move early. She was one of them, and I thought, *Okay, I'll just hit the ball into the other side of the net.* Got it.

There weren't any more misses by either team, though there was some drama. As Kara Lang was stepping up to take her shot, the Brazilian keeper kicked the ball away, which wasn't cool. Kara retrieved it, walked to the spot and buried it.

Sasha Andrews scored the winner for us. I had never seen her take a PK before, but that day she had this extreme confidence. Everything about her said *I'm going to score—* and, sure enough, she did. It was the perfect storybook ending, too, because Edmonton is her hometown.

We were into the final, which drew an even bigger crowd to the stadium. But it didn't go quite as planned. We took the Americans to extra time before losing 1–0.

Still, that's one tournament where even though we didn't win, I was so proud of us. I remember Kara, who was only fifteen, absolutely bawling on the field after-wards. And I said to her, "Look at the fans. Look at the stands. We did this. We have nothing to cry about."

Oh, wise one, me . . .

It was one of those moments where, yes, we lost, but it truly felt like a bunch of teenagers had changed the sport. I had a decent tournament, and finished as the leading goal scorer, but what sticks out in my memory is all those fans coming out in Edmonton and us thinking that we'd arrived, that soccer in Canada had arrived, and that there was no turning back.

Of course, all that soccer action unfolded a lot more slowly than I thought it was going to back then. But at least we showed that Canada really was a soccer country—it just needed an opportunity to come watch.

After the tournament, I went back to Portland for my sophomore year. I guess Canada wasn't the only place where they were paying attention to what had happened in the tournament. I remember my UP teammates coming up to me and saying, "*Oh, my God!*" They were blown away.

And Clive said, "I knew you had it in you." That was him.

It breaks my heart that I only had two years with Clive. I never had a coach who cared so much about people as people. He never boasted about his relationships with the best players on his teams because he always said they were going to be stars no matter what he did with them. He prided himself on seeing where he could take freshmen who came into the program with unrealized potential. He knew only a handful would ever make a national or pro team, but he really cared about the development of players and putting them on a path for success as a person.

And we really cared about Clive, who had recently been diagnosed with prostate cancer. The prognosis wasn't good.

That season he was in and out with us. He lost his hair because of chemo and lost a lot of weight, and he was sick to the point where we didn't know if he would be able to continue as our coach. But he hardly missed a day, even when he had to come around in a golf cart instead of jogging across the field like he used to.

There were obviously some challenges. He couldn't make some of the road trips. But we had a great season, won our playoff bracket, and made it to the national championship tournament in Austin, Texas. We were the eighth seed of the eight teams there, but we played hard and made it to the national final against Santa Clara, who were our great rivals in the West Coast Conference.

Before that final game, we were all stressed. When we went out on the field for practice, Clive said, "All right, everyone. Take off your boots."

"Uh okay . . ."

"This is our practice today," Clive said. "I want to see who can throw their soccer boots the farthest."

And that was practice. That was it. We all took turns throwing our boots. Honestly, to this day, I don't think I played in my own boots in the final game. Everyone had the same kind and, after we were done throwing them, we all just grabbed ones that fit.

I don't think a lot of coaches, playing for a national championship, would have handled the situation that way. It broke the tension. It relaxed us.

—

There are a few things that stand out about that game. Yes, I scored a couple of goals. Woo! But what I really remember is how our team rallied to achieve something and just refused to lose.

The game was tied 1–1 in extra time when our all-star keeper, Lauren Arase—such a stud—got kicked in the face and had to be taken off on a stretcher. Our other keeper was a freshman, Kim Head, who hadn't been on the field all season. Now here she was, being thrown into extra time in a national championship game.

I remember our captain, Lauren Orlando, bringing the team in and saying, "We are not giving up a shot. We are not losing this game."

Then Kristen Moore and I connected on the winning goal. She was my roommate in freshman and sophomore year, so that was pretty cool. Two small schools playing for a national championship was also cool, as was us beating our conference rivals in extra time: it was kind of perfect how it all played out.

People are always asking me to name the best moment I have experienced on a soccer field. They're surprised to find out that number one is winning the national championship for Clive Charles and seeing him hug the trophy that day.

It was so much bigger than sport.

That was the last game Clive ever coached.

—

I decided to redshirt my junior year; in the US college system, if you "redshirt," you sit out a year, but you retain a year of eligibility to keep playing at the university level. I wanted to be able to concentrate on the World Cup, which was coming up in the early fall of 2003, right in the middle of the college season. If I stayed on the roster, I would have to miss a month and a half of college games, which didn't seem right. And there was also school, which I would also have to sit out as a red shirt wishing to retain eligibility. I was a biology major. I cared about my grades and how I did in school, and the decision about the academic break was just as tough.

I remember being so nervous about telling Clive that I put it off. And I put it off some more. Finally, he called me into the office and said, "Look, I can only imagine what you're going through. We're going to redshirt you next year." Thank God!

I still had to have some hard conversations with teammates who were going into their senior year, telling them, "Sorry, I'm not going to be here for you right after we won a championship together." Such a tough call.

Something major changed during that redshirt year. When someone asks me now where my home is, I still say "Burnaby." But 2003 to 2004 was the first time I had lived in Portland while not going to school. I still trained with the university team between my national team camps, but that was it.

And that's when Portland also became home for me. It still is. I bonded with the city that year.

Portland feels a lot like Vancouver or Seattle. It's a little smaller, but it has the same environment, the same types of people, the same energy. It's relaxed and isn't such a fast-paced place. I have spent time living in California and Western New York while I played on professional teams there, and I can vouch that life is slower here in Portland. Plus, there's great coffee, great food. It is close enough to home but—especially during those first years—also far enough away from home.

And it pains me to say this, but there just aren't options for female athletes to work in Canada.

As soon as I graduated from UP I got my green card, because I knew that there was going to be a professional league in the United States before there was one in Canada. Not that everything's about your work and job, but as a player who lives to play there was nothing for me in Canada.

Clive Charles passed away in August 2003, a few weeks before the beginning of the World Cup.

When he died, it felt like the whole Portland university and soccer community grieved together. The school held a memorial service for him, and the number of people there was overwhelming. My whole family came down from Canada. There was such a sense of people rallying around each other, especially the players on our UP team, who had already experienced a lot of highs and lows (including when one of my teammates lost her mom on 9/11).

Looking back, I think the greatest testimony to Clive is the number of people who came to play for the University of Portland while he was coaching and then never left the city. Portland became their home, and many of them stayed involved in the game. (I've noticed that when coaches really have a positive impact, their players tend to stick around the sport when their careers are done, like the members of our 2012 Olympic team under John Herdman. If players have poor experiences with a coach the opposite is true—they get the heck out as soon as they can.)

Clive's legacy is obvious. Garrett Smith—who had been Clive's assistant coach for a year, and before that had played for him at UP—took over the women's program after Clive died. It was such a smooth transition. Garrett wasn't Clive and he was never going to be, but it did feel like there was continuity. Michelle French, who also played at UP, is the coach there now. That sense of community and pride that Clive built is still alive twenty years later.

Winning the national college championship in 2002 helped us recruit some really good players, including

Megan Rapinoe, Steph Cox, Angie Woznuk and Lindsey Huie, who all went on to play for the US national team.

It would never be the same as when Clive was alive and coaching, but the program was in good hands.

I guess I'm part of Clive's legacy as well. I'm one of those people who stuck around.

6

FOURTH IN THE WORLD CUP. WHAT'S THE PROBLEM?

The 2003 World Cup was my first big senior tournament for Canada. Even gave a bunch of us youngsters a chance to play, and he also kept veterans such as Charmaine Hooper, Silvana Burtini and Andrea Neil, because they were so amazing. The tournament was originally scheduled to take place in China but was moved to the United States after the SARS epidemic emerged in Asia in February and then spread. I have to credit the US and its federation, because they were the only country that could have possibly put together a World Cup on such a tight timeline. Obviously, it wasn't the same as the 1999 World Cup, but it was a miracle that it even came off.

I was still a kid, and I admit I didn't really understand the sacrifice and work it took to get to a World Cup. I was just enjoying the ride. There was no pressure on the young players, and there was no real pressure on Canada. After the disappointing result four years earlier, we weren't expected to do well at all.

We were a physical team, a group of big, strong athletes. If you weren't at least five eight, and fast, you'd struggle trying to play with us. Except for Diana Matheson, of course, who was just over five feet.

Even liked a very direct, very low-risk style of soccer. Get the ball as far away from our goal and as close to their goal as quickly as possible. You worked hard for each other, and you didn't make it fun for the opposition. It wasn't the prettiest football, and it might not have been so enjoyable to watch, but back in the early 2000s, it was a very successful way of playing the women's game. I don't know if our midfielders enjoyed it that much either, because they never touched the ball. Not everyone we played against was super organized, so we could be successful by just being athletic and imposing ourselves.

I thrived doing that. Just knock the ball up to me and Charmaine and Christine Latham and Silvana, and we would feed off it.

The truth is, we did pretty well by playing that way. I'm not giving anything away to leap ahead here and say we finished fourth, which remains the best World Cup result Canada's women's team has ever had.

—

That was one of the first tournaments where we worked on team culture and off-field connections. As one of the veterans of the team, Andrea Neil took the lead in a lot of that. I can only assume that was because Even and the team's staff realized the environment and culture hadn't been the greatest at the World Cup in 1999, where the results had been so terrible.

We had a residency camp in Vancouver for four or five months leading up to the tournament in late September and October. We trained with a guy named Peter Twist, who had worked with male hockey players. I remember putting in a lot of hard days and feeling a lot of fatigue. That kind of heavy training also helped us form connections and bonds, and I think those bonds benefited us in the tournament, where we had to rely on each other and turn to each other and support each other.

But there's no denying that our team was a work in progress. Some of the veterans were angry and rightfully so. The national team had experienced *no* success to that point and had enjoyed very limited support. And there was a big age gap between the vets and the naive new kids on the squad, like me and Erin and Diana.

This was the last major tournament for Silvana, Andrea, Charmaine and Sharolta. Not all of them wanted to retire. Some of them were pushed out by the big group of kids coming in. The younger players on that World Cup team are still some of my best friends. But I don't keep in touch with the veterans.

And maybe that kind of showed. The divide wasn't drastic. It was just two different groups of players with different experiences and backgrounds. There was a bunch of kids thinking, *This is amazing, I've been on the national team for three years, I've played in a World Cup, we finished fourth—what's the problem?*

But those older players hadn't experienced things the way we had. I have the utmost respect for all of them. And I am so thankful for all of them. Charmaine and Silvana and other veterans built the program when there was nothing. I also give Even a lot of credit for demanding funding and support from the CSA—and demanding residency camps and opportunities to play games that the team had never had before.

Even and those players changed the entire trajectory of the program. They deserve so much credit.

Our first match was against Germany. I remember walking by their players before the game and thinking, *Oh my gosh—the strength and size and power!* I had never seen an entire team of such obvious athletes, who were also such incredibly gifted soccer players.

The game started and I scored in the fourth minute to put us up 1–0. For about a second, it felt easy.

Then reality hit. Germany destroyed us. We lost 4–1.

We rebounded very well and beat Argentina in our

second match, which meant that we had to beat Japan in our third game to get out of the group. They were an up-and-coming team back then, not the power they would become in a few years. We beat them 3–1 at Giants Stadium to advance to the quarterfinal against China.

That match was in Portland, in the same stadium where I had watched the 1999 World Cup, and here I was playing in one. It's kind of weird how things happen sometimes. All my teammates from UP were in the stands, and a bunch of my family came down. Charmaine scored an early goal, and that was it: we won 1–0 to reach the semifinal against Sweden.

What I will always remember about that semifinal match is that we *had* them. We were up 1–0 after Kara scored a goal in the second half. Then they tied it late, and a few minutes later they scored off a quick free kick when we didn't get set up defensively in time. Game over.

Of course, I was upset and disappointed. But I was so young I didn't really understand what a big deal the loss was. You just assume you'll have another chance someday. But imagine playing in a World Cup final. We'd had the chance to win a World Cup. It would have been massive. And then in a few seconds, we lost it. And we've never been that close again.

The other semifinal had been played in the same stadium in Portland right before our match. That was a game that really shook the foundations of women's soccer. It was the

Americans against Germany, and the US team still had most of the stars who'd put the women's game on the map by winning the World Cup in 1999.

I remember watching from the sideline as the Germans absolutely dominated the Americans, winning 3–0. In that moment, we all saw how the women's game was growing. Germany and Sweden were headed for the World Cup final, and the US was out. It was a shock and a statement and it solidified Germany's place in the women's game for the next fifteen years. Suddenly, losing 4–1 to Germany in the opening game didn't look so bad.

For the longest time, the US had dominated women's soccer because they were good at the game, but also because they were athletically superior to everyone they played. With Germany in 2003, the US finally came up against a team that was athletically superior to them, and they got played off the park.

Germany beat Sweden in the final. We played the Americans in the third-place game.

I remember scoring to tie the game 1–1, but they came out flying. The final score was 3–1. With the (possible) exception of Sweden, the teams we lost to in that tournament simply outplayed us. The US was just that much better than we were. We could hang in and not lose 9–1 like we used to, but we still had a ways to go.

There was a huge difference between this World Cup experience and the disaster the veterans had experienced in 1999. The team was moving in the right direction and had shown vast improvements. The future seemed bright with Even as our head coach. We were no longer a pushover. That tournament showed that we had arrived on the world stage. We were only going to get better.

But there would be a few rough years for the national team after that World Cup success.

Women's soccer had become part of the Olympics in 1996. Qualification for the Atlanta Games in 1996 and Sydney in 2000—both only eight-team tournaments—was based on the results of the 1995 and 1999 World Cups, respectively, so Canada didn't make it.

But for the 2004 Olympics in Athens, there was a proper qualifying tournament for countries in our region, which is known as CONCACAF. The top two teams from North America and Central America would qualify. The Americans were a lock for one of those places; if we could make it to the semifinals, we would be going to the Olympics.

The tournament was played in Costa Rica. In three group-stage games, we beat Jamaica, Panama and Costa Rica by a cumulative score of 14–1. That put us into the semifinal against Mexico.

We had never lost to Mexico before. We haven't lost to Mexico since.

I remember being in our team hotel before the match, and our phones were ringing all night, and drums were banging outside our windows. That's CONCACAF for you. It wasn't pleasant.

And then we went out the next day and lost. That was one of the lowest lows of my career. It was devastating for all of us. With the World Cup result in 2003, we just assumed we would be playing in the next Olympics. And once you make it to the Olympics, you're an Olympian forever.

I remember thinking that this chance might never come again. It was absolutely brutal.

That was a transitional time for the national team. A lot of the older players had gone. Those of us who had been eighteen or nineteen in the 2003 World Cup were now the "veterans" on the team, and we started to feel the pressure to get results and the pressure to perform. We were no longer just the kids who could show up and enjoy ourselves. This loss hurt because now *we* were the ones who had failed.

We had also become a little stagnant as a team. I don't really know why. It's one of those things in sport that you can't really explain. It's not that your team or your players have gotten worse. But for some reason you lose an important game that you should have won.

It didn't feel like we were suddenly awful or that we were never going to rebound. It didn't feel like panic. We were still making progress. But when you finish fourth in a World Cup, everyone assumes you're good. And then you lose a match to Mexico and don't qualify for the Olympics, and people naturally start wondering if maybe the World Cup was the outlier. Maybe the wins were the outliers, not the loss.

Between 2000 and 2005 a lot of new players made their national team debuts, and a lot of veterans left the program. Even brought in so many players for their first caps. He gave everyone a chance. But if you were a new player joining the national team in 2005, say, the veterans were me and Erin McLeod, and we were only twenty-three. It was a little different.

We were hoping to evolve as a team more quickly. The women's game and the players had changed a lot since Even had won an Olympic gold medal coaching Norway. But we were still playing that direct, long-ball, safety-first style. Defend, defend. The players who were coming onto the national team were more technically gifted and wanted to be able to play a more skills-oriented style. That tension was starting to creep into the team, and it was undermining.

Garrett Smith tried to talk me into coming back to the University of Portland after the World Cup to play the last part of the 2003 college season. I'm so glad I didn't do that, because if I had, I wouldn't have been able to play my senior season in 2005.

I'd take our 2005 UP team against any college team that has ever played. It all just worked out perfectly in terms of players coming back, like me, and players coming in who had all redshirted their freshman year to play in the Youth World Cup—Megan Rapinoe and Steph Cox and Angie Woznuk. When all of us played together, we were unstoppable. It was so much fun. We had the time of our lives.

The team came together for the first time in the spring of 2005. We played an exhibition game against the Mexican national team, and we killed them. I remember thinking, *Oh my gosh, we're just going to destroy college teams.* And we did.

When we went down to the University of Oregon for a match, their coach decided to re-line the field to make it as small as possible, thinking that was going to stop us because it would be easier to defend. We beat them 6–0.

There were some bumps along the way but not many— we won every game that season. I took summer classes, so I was in school, but I had pretty much already finished my major and minor, including the hardest courses I had to take. I was playing soccer on a historically great team, going to a few classes, and having a blast. I wish everyone could have a last semester like that.

In the first game of the Final Four we were matched against Penn State. It was one of our tougher games of the year and went to penalties. I was shooting fifth, and Penn State's keeper was my friend and teammate from the Canadian national team, Erin McLeod.

I scored, and we won.

We played UCLA in the championship game. My college career had kind of come full circle, because UCLA was the first team I'd played as a freshman. We lost that time, but we weren't going to lose this one.

UCLA was the up-and-coming program, with the new cool kids. During the buildup to the game, the hype was all about them.

Then we came out and we dominated. We were up 3–0 at the half. I will never forget a reporter interviewing Garrett at halftime. "How do you think UCLA feels at this moment?" she asked him.

"UCLA?" Garrett replied. "Didn't you just see the University of Portland demolish them?"

It was so funny.

We ended up winning 4–0. It was the perfect capper to my college days, and one of those rare years where nothing could go wrong. Bringing another national championship back home to Portland meant so much, especially to the seniors who were ending their careers with a victory.

It was one of the most magical runs of my life.

7

HOLY BLEEP! WE QUALIFIED FOR THE OLYMPICS!

In 2003, the first professional women's soccer league in North America, the Women's United Soccer Association (WUSA), folded. My plan had been to turn pro after I graduated, but the league was gone. I'm sure there were options in Europe, but it wasn't like they were out searching for players in North America the way they are now.

At least I had the national team to pick up the slack. In the lead-up to the 2007 World Cup in China, we were given the chance to live in a residency in Vancouver for a year and a half and train full-time. I played for the Vancouver Whitecaps women's team in the summer, but otherwise I was with the national team full-time.

I believe Greg Kerfoot, the Whitecaps' owner, was the one who put up the money for the residency, for which I, and the whole program, will be forever grateful. I think there was an understanding that if there hadn't been a residency, a lot of the players on the national team might have had to leave the sport and find a real job. It saved some careers.

They put us up in apartments close to downtown Vancouver; I roomed with Rhian Wilkinson. We had some "carding" funding from the government, money earmarked to support Canadian athletes who compete internationally, and I'd signed a Nike deal after I graduated. It was the first time I was able to earn money playing soccer. I was getting to play every day, I lived rent-free and was given a car to drive. For someone who had just graduated from college, it wasn't a bad life.

And even though the apartment we were living in was supposed to be pet-free, I smuggled in a puppy in my backpack. That was my first dog.

The 2007 World Cup in China is kind of a blur for me, maybe because it was a complete failure.

There was a big women's soccer tournament in China every year, so I was very familiar with playing there. By the time the 2007 World Cup came around I'd probably been to China four times already. It's a difficult place to play, and I think it's a difficult place for many North American players to stay for a long period of time. Athletes are truly creatures of habit, right down to the food they eat. It's incredible to be able to see other parts of the world, but sometimes having to deal with so much cultural difference is not ideal for competition.

In our first group match, we lost to Norway. Candace Chapman got the opening goal for us, but they scored twice in the second half. Then we beat Ghana 4–0; I scored a couple of goals in that one.

The killer was our final group match against Australia. With a win we would have gone through to the knockout stages.

Melissa Tancredi—whose nickname, justifiably, was Tanc—scored in the first minute to put us ahead. Australia equalized after the half. Then I scored a late goal that looked like the winner, but they tied it two minutes into added time at the end of the match, and that was it.

Germany won that World Cup, beating Brazil in the final, after Brazil knocked out the Americans 4–0 in the semifinal.

But I have pretty much erased that tournament from my memory.

The qualifying tournament for the Beijing Olympics was held in Juárez, Mexico, in April 2008. That was . . . an experience. To this day I question why the qualifiers were in Juárez. A Mexican border town across from El Paso, Texas, Juárez is a notoriously dangerous, intimidating place. There were security guards everywhere we went. For safety reasons, we weren't allowed to leave the hotel. Once, we took the bus from training to the only Starbucks in town because we weren't allowed to go by ourselves. In order to train, we walked across the border into the United States. That was unique.

Playing in an Olympic gold medal final is nowhere near as stressful as playing in an Olympic qualifying tournament—at least for me. That was especially true after the heartbreak of our previous qualifying attempt. We realized then that even if you knew you should qualify, it was possible to not qualify. Until we lost to Mexico, we'd never thought we wouldn't go through.

And now we were playing in Mexico, dealing with hostile fans, with the dangers of Juárez, with a bunch of different challenges. The scenario unfolded exactly as it had the last time: we were set to play Mexico in the semi-final. The winner would go to the Olympics. The loser was out.

It was another nail-biter. Tanc stood on her head in that tournament and scored a boatload of goals. She scored first, and then we worked to protect our lead. I remember that, in the final minutes, Even wanted to move me to centre back to shore up the defence.

I turned to him and said, "Do you *want* to win this game?"

He thought better of it, which was a good thing. I am definitely not a natural defender.

I remember what it felt like when the final whistle blew and we knew that we had qualified, that we were going to be Olympians.

Growing up, for me and my brother it was all about the Olympics. You can't take that out of me. For the longest time going to the Olympics had been one of my goals—it's different than playing in the World Cup, even though the World Cup is the biggest event in our sport.

For the Canadian women's team, qualifying for the World Cup should never be an issue, because four teams are accepted from our region; since we consistently rank in the top ten in the world, we should have no trouble being one of them. But for the Olympics, there's the stress of that one game that decides whether you are in or out.

And everyone knows the Olympics—not just soccer fans. So many of us grow up watching the games and remember the first time they saw a Canadian athlete win gold. When that match against Mexico ended, I flashed forward to what I now had the opportunity to be a part of. The Olympic Village. The opening and closing ceremonies. The Team Canada gear. I would be representing my country along with all the other Canadian athletes from all those different sports.

Once we qualified, it was *Holy bleep!* It was *Holy xxxx! I'm going to be part of it. I get to represent Canada in an Olympic Games!*

Heading for China, we felt like an up-and-coming team teetering on the edge of being really good. Did we expect to beat the US and Germany? No. But could we? Yes. By then we definitely weren't getting played off the park. In every game we were going to be competitive. Every game was going to be a battle.

What a whirlwind that trip was. The China of those Olympics didn't feel like the country I had experienced before. There was blue sky! (You might remember that China shut down all the factories around Beijing during the Olympics to get rid of the air pollution.)

The first highlight was walking into the Olympic Village, which was just out of this world. I guess you could tell we were all first-time Olympians given how wide-eyed we were at everything. Walking for miles and miles around the Olympic Village is probably not the best use of your energy before a competition, but we wanted to experience everything.

We played well the whole tournament. We beat Argentina, then tied China, which meant that we were guaranteed a spot in the quarterfinals no matter what happened in our final group game against Sweden, which we ended up losing 2–1. Every game was close. I don't think we were expecting to win gold. It was more a case of "Let's get out of our group and see what happens."

Of course, we drew the Americans in the quarterfinals in Shanghai. Heading in, I thought we had a legitimate shot against them.

It was a crazy night. Thunderstorms forced organizers to pause the game for almost an hour and a half. Then Erin took a bad step in goal and tore her ACL. She tried to keep playing even with the torn ligament—if that's not crazy I don't know what is—but eventually she couldn't continue, and they brought in Karina to replace her.

The Americans scored first and then I scored after the thunderstorm to tie it.

It went into extra time and felt like we were going to penalties. Then the Americans scored the winner in the 101st minute.

We were upset and mad and disappointed because we wouldn't have the chance to play for a medal, but we also realized that we had done pretty well in our first Olympic Games.

I much prefer being at an Olympics where I *don't* have the opportunity to watch other events, because that means my team has been successful in the tournament and I'm busy playing until the very last day. But we got to be tourists in Beijing after we lost to the Americans, and it was a blast. We went to all kinds of other events—beach volleyball, the men's soccer final, track and field at the Bird's Nest stadium. To this day, it remains the only Olympics where we got to cheer on other Canadian athletes.

Then we went to the closing ceremonies. I was in awe the entire time—and I even have pictures of me and Chinese basketball legend Yao Ming, all seven feet six inches of him. We had worked hard and long to get there, and then everyone had the chance to let their guard down. It was just one big party.

But there was another feeling running through the party as well.

Even's contract was up after the Olympics. We knew he had coached his last game with us and would be heading home to Norway. We were a little afraid of who might come next. But we were also excited to think about where someone new might take us.

Still, Even Pellerud was the only national team coach I had known. What if the new coach didn't like how I played? What if they completely changed everything? It could go well—or not so well.

I credit where I am today as a soccer player to Even. He was the coach who took a chance on a bunch of sixteen-year-olds, and we all owe him thanks for that. But I think he was done in 2008. The Beijing Olympics was it. He had been around for eight or nine years, and national team coaches don't typically stick around for that long.

Even had done his job. He put us on the map in terms of woman's football. We'd finished fourth at a World Cup. We'd qualified for the Olympics. None of that had happened before for Canada. But it was time for the program to move on.

I think the players all assumed that Ian Bridge, Even's assistant, was going to take over. He seemed like the logical next step: he was Canadian, he knew us and he was the coach of the youth programs. We all loved Ian and were really looking forward to working with him.

And then Carolina Morace was named our new head coach.

There wasn't any consultation with the players about the hiring. I don't know if players having a voice in the hiring of a coach is a good thing or a bad thing. I don't fully understand the process of how the CSA hires coaches.

The association just announces who it's going to be. That was the case with John Herdman, too, and Kenneth Heiner-Møller and Bev Priestman, who came after him.

The thing is, as a player you're not on the national team because you signed a four-year contract, like you do in the pros. You have to earn your place every day. If the CSA wants to know what players think, they tend to ask retired ones, not the players who are currently on the team.

I got the news of Carolina's hiring in an e-mail sent by the CSA and remember I was excited. I had obviously heard of Carolina, who'd been a very successful player for Italy. I was a little disappointed Ian didn't get the job, because I really liked him, but I was excited to play for a female head coach for the first time. I thought she was someone who could help us progress in our style of play. I did wonder if Carolina knew what she was getting into, given the battle all our coaches seem to have to go through with the CSA for funding and budget. I didn't actually think about what we players were about to get into.

8

A BROKEN NOSE WASN'T THE WORST OF IT

We had our first camp with Carolina in the Los Angeles area just after she became our coach, in February 2009. It was obvious right from the start that there was a cultural gulf between her and the Canadian team, starting with the language barrier. Carolina had a translator with her. Her entire staff was Italian, including the team doctor. I remember thinking, *Well, this is going to require an adjustment.* Even ended up spending eight or nine years in Canada and kind of evolved into a Canadian over that time. A little more indirect, a little less blunt, a little more diplomatic, a little more nice. And now here were all these Italians who were very upfront, very direct, very strict. There were no filters on what they said to you.

For instance, they had no problem telling you to your face that you were fat. They were really focused on weight. During team meetings they posted everyone's weight—how much weight a person had gained or lost, and what their ideal weight should be. All of that for everyone to see. If the staff decided you weren't fit enough, you had to do push-ups on the hotel swimming pool deck and touch your nose into the water. That was before breakfast.

In Italy, this was apparently just the normal way team athletes were treated. But it was a big shift for all of us. So was Carolina's training methodology. I actually loved her practices. Everything was soccer specific. She focused us on movement and trying to become better athletes, on coordination and agility and other stuff that we had never been exposed to before. I didn't love players being told that they were fat, and other things like that. But those hours on the field were incredible.

In hindsight, there were other early red flags. Staff conducted room raids to see if you had any candy or sweets. They would knock on your door, and after you opened it, they would walk in and have a look around. I remember one night around eight o'clock I was sitting with a Gatorade when they did their room check. "You shouldn't be drinking that this late," I was told. "You should only be drinking water."

One of our players had come from Sweden and brought Swedish fish candy and a bunch of other treats with her. As word of the room raids spread, the message was: "Hide your candy." That player picked up all her goodies, brought them into the shower with her, and turned on the water, figuring the staff wasn't going to search her in the stall.

All of that happened during the first camp. I remember thinking, *Okay, so this is different.*

Carolina is passionate about soccer. I would say she's one of the most passionate people I've ever met when it comes to the game. She has strong ideas about how it should be played and how players should perform. She's very intense. Maybe it was just her nature or maybe soccer is life and death for all Italians in the sport.

She also has a sarcastic and funny side she showed at times, but I don't think many people outside of our team bubble got to see that. She's one of those people who walks into a room and just commands it.

Looking back, I think the players, and even the CSA, got—well, maybe not brainwashed, because that's such a harsh word—but got caught up in Carolina's mystique.

For starters, we all moved to Italy to train because that's what Carolina wanted. Think of that: the Canadian women's soccer team was training in Italy.

At the time I remember saying to myself, *Okay, this is going to be hard, but we'll do it because the coach says we should do it.*

There have been a few times during my career when my desire to win for my country, my love of the game, my love of representing Canada, my desire to play at World Cups and in the Olympics, made me willing to sacrifice some things that, looking back, I shouldn't have. And it wasn't just me who made such sacrifices.

I really can't figure out why *any* of us thought that moving the Canadian national team to Rome was a good idea. It blows my mind now. I don't know why the CSA allowed it. I don't know why, as players, we jumped on the plane and went along with it. Because it was rough.

We were told that if we were based out of Europe during the buildup to the 2011 World Cup in Germany, we would be able to play a lot more games with much less travel. "Yeah, that sounds great," we all said. "That makes sense."

We ended up playing something like three games the whole time we were over there.

But we accepted what we were told because that was the vibe of the team. Just like me, the other players on the national team were ready to do anything to wear that jersey representing Canada and to play in World Cups. You weren't playing for Team Canada to make millions of dollars. It was strictly about your passion for the game and your connection to the other players. That has always been our X factor, but it was even more so back then.

We were a close-knit team, and moving to Italy did make us even closer and tighter, because we were all in it together. But it wasn't a good situation.

Friends and family members would say, "Oh you're so lucky to be spending three months in Rome."

Are you kidding?

We lived in the Hotel Mancini. It wasn't the nicest. There was one room we called the "animal room." As I remember, that's where Kaylyn Kyle had to stay. We were convinced it had rats. You could hear their claws scrabbling in the walls.

The hotel was designed for the professional soccer teams that came to play in Rome. For instance, men's teams would stay there if they had a game with AS Roma in Serie A. They'd be there for a night or two and it was perfect for them. There was a gym and a soccer field and a pool. It was a little ways away from Rome, to help staff keep the players out of the city.

But to live there for weeks and weeks on end was a different story. It wasn't the worst, but it wasn't like you were living at some grand hotel. At least the food was on point—it was Italy, after all. Karina LeBlanc hoarded extra pesto from the meals in her room, she loved it so much.

But it was very isolating. The area around the hotel was a mixture of country and suburbs. There were a couple of stores. It wasn't like we were out on a farm all by ourselves, but we were stuck a long way from anywhere interesting.

It took a lot of negotiating for us to eventually get three team rental cars so that we could at least go into Rome on off days. But none of us understood the parking rules. After the fact, Carolina got sent parking fines amounting to thousands of dollars because we had parked randomly around Rome, accumulating all these parking tickets.

She wasn't happy about that.

And I will always remember the crappy internet. We were away from our families and reaching out to them over the internet was our main means of communication. It got to the point where a few of us would go across the street to a different hotel and hang out in the lobby to steal their signal. The staff couldn't even get our only connection to home right.

We were confined to the hotel for a month at a stretch. Then individual players were allowed to go away for a little break, as long as they came right back. A lot of players visited Naples and Venice and saw other amazing places.

But it was just . . . a lot.

We had our first camp in Italy in 2010. In 2011, we were there from February until the World Cup that summer. Candace Chapman and I decided we wanted to play pro in the US, and we managed to convince Carolina and the staff that it would be better preparation for us to play two games a week with a pro team than to stay in Italy. But we were definitely frowned upon. I played for the Western New York Flash just outside of Buffalo. I'd be in Buffalo for ten days and then have to fly back to Rome for two weeks.

Looking back, I think about the fact that a coach tried her best to prevent people from playing professionally because she wanted to keep them in a residency environment far away from home. If that wasn't a warning sign, I don't know what was.

—

Our regular routine in camp was that we would wake up, eat breakfast at the restaurant within the hotel and then train in the morning. Then came lunch, followed in the afternoon, depending on what day it was, by a gym session, and then dinner and that was it. There was a lot of down time.

Camps nowadays are ten days at most, and it's a very busy ten days because the time is limited. In Italy we didn't really have meetings or film sessions; that's because we weren't preparing for a game or reviewing a game—we were just living. We didn't have evening meetings or one-on-one meetings with the coach or her staff. Even when we got to the World Cup, we still didn't do film sessions. We still didn't analyze practices.

But, even so, we were playing great soccer under Carolina. FIFA had never ranked us higher as a team. We won CONCACAF. We won the Algarve Cup. Part of that goes back to just how close we became as a team—we were doing it for each other. But I also have to give Carolina credit for how she evolved the way we played. She created real soccer players out of a group who, under Even, just booted the ball and chased it.

So it was strange.

Don't get me wrong: there were cool moments in Italy. There were aspects of our time there that felt like a once in a lifetime opportunity. We went to see the Colosseum, for one. I found it so fascinating that I went back two more times. I also got to the point where I knew where I was in the city.

But we weren't the Italian national team. And we weren't home.

Before the 2011 World Cup started, all of us had been at the camp in Italy for a month, which is a long buildup. That's something we've learned since as a team: when we do a long camp right before a World Cup, we've never been successful. The World Cup itself is so long that by the time you're entering the knockout stages you've been together for two months straight. We kind of nailed the Olympic tournament and how to be successful there, but how do you do it when the tournament is three times as long?

As the opening match loomed, we were more than ready to get to Germany. There was a different buzz there, and it was refreshing. I remember arriving in Berlin and thinking, *All right, this is why we did all that work.* The Germans got all the little things about hosting a World Cup right. For instance, we showed up to a bus painted in the Team Canada colours. For the first time, it felt like we were having a tournament like the ones you see on TV—the ones for the men, I mean. That's what it was like.

And we were playing so well. But we also hadn't played that many games.

We were in a group with Germany, France and Nigeria. The chatter was that it was a toss-up between us and Germany as to who was the favourite to finish first.

We were confident. We were ready to go. Honestly, I was thinking semifinal, final—that's where we're headed.

Just after we got to Germany, we had a celebration for Karina because it was her fourth World Cup. To that point, no player in Canadian history had done that. We all went out and sang karaoke. And, finally, we were able to see friends and family, who had come over for the tournament. I remember going out for coffee with Rhian Wilkinson's family and Diana Matheson's family. Some of my own family came too.

So, we went from being isolated for weeks to being totally scattered. I had never spent so much time outside the team hotel in the days before a World Cup. I admit it felt liberating to no longer be relying on my teammates for everything. But I think, in those few days, we lost some of our tight-knittedness as a team.

The day before the opening game, we drove to the Olympic Stadium and had our practice there. There's something about the last training session the day before a World Cup opens or an Olympics starts. I remember being nervous and feeling that sense of anticipation. There's nothing that compares to it. And this wasn't just any stadium, but the Berlin Olympic Stadium, with all that history.

And then came the game.

Having now played under John Herdman, Kenneth Heiner-Møller and Bev Priestman—all of whom were determined that Canada would be the most prepared team in the stadium for each and every game—I can look back and understand that, under Carolina, we weren't the least bit ready for the actual games, for our opponents, for what happens when you're down 1–0 after ten minutes.

We had spent all this time together, yet when it came to the crunch, we weren't anywhere near as prepared as we could have been. Not that I realized that at the time. It only became apparent as our tournament—our very short tournament—transpired.

We had one way of playing. We had one formation. We had one style. That was it. If it wasn't working, the coach's answer was that we had to do it better. Which just doesn't work.

With John and the coaches after him, if something wasn't working, we'd switch formation and try something new. We didn't have that option at the World Cup in Germany.

It was so intimidating walking into the stadium for that first match. Nadine Angerer was the goalkeeper for the German team. I would play with her later on the Portland Thorns, where we became best friends. We still talk about this game all the time.

At the stadium, we came out of the locker room and lined up behind what looked like a garage door. You couldn't see into the stadium. You could just hear it. The roar of the crowd. It was on a scale that I'd never experienced before and have yet to experience again.

Then they lifted the door and I pooped my pants (figuratively).

It was that loud.

Male players at the world level experience that roar all the time. It's obviously not always as intense as at the World Cup, but even in their club games they're playing in front of fifty to sixty thousand fans. Female players are almost never in that position. To have that door go up and to see that mass of people—I don't even know how many there were. Only that the stadium was sold out and filled with screaming German fans.

It made me feel an inch tall. Like I was just so tiny. Like we were playing against an entire country, and every one of its citizens was in those stands watching. And then we had to listen to the whole crowd sing the German national anthem while it was just our team singing "O Canada."

But when the whistle blew, the fans disappeared, the noise disappeared. I felt other kinds of nerves and anticipation because of the significance of the match, but it's amazing what your brain can do to shut stuff out.

Looking back, we did okay, given the circumstances. We lost 2–1, but I was proud of the way we performed. There's not a more difficult game to play than the opener of a World Cup against the host country—in this case facing potentially the best team in the world.

We gave up a goal early. But we fought back. We did what Canadians do. We dug in and defended for our lives and created the odd chance, even with everything stacked against us.

If someone had told me heading into that game that we were going to lose 2–1, I would have thought, *That sucks, but we can handle it*—especially given that it was supposed to be the toughest matchup in our group.

But it wasn't just losing the match. Sometimes other shit happens, like breaking my nose.

That's not how you want to start a World Cup, and it wasn't exactly a good sign in terms of what was to come. Injuries happen, freak things happen. But it still sucks, given how much time you spend trying to be as fit and healthy as you can be.

I've seen the video. I definitely took an elbow in the face before I went down—where was VAR when I needed it?

The physio and the doctor ran out on the field. I still had my head down, and they asked me, "What's wrong?"

"I broke my nose," I said. It really didn't hurt that much, but I could feel it crunch and I could sense that it wasn't straight.

Without even having to look that closely, they said, in unison, "Yeah, you did."

If you have to break your nose, I think it was as good a break as you could get on the soccer field. It didn't bleed. It wasn't that painful. It was just . . . crooked.

I wasn't thinking about coming out of the game, but if the medical people come out to look at you, the rules say you have to come off the field temporarily. Then our doctors told me I couldn't go back out.

It was the World Cup. I wasn't sitting out because my nose was a little bent.

Canadians would have gotten what I was saying. But those Italian doctors thought I was the craziest person for wanting to go back on, I guess because they come from a background in soccer where players roll around like they've been shot after they get their foot stepped on.

I insisted, and finally they agreed to let me go back out, saying, "Try not to get hit in the head again."

I scored a late goal to make it 2–1, and our team came off the field feeling pretty positive about ourselves despite the loss.

After the game, I went to the hospital and they reset my nose as best they could. That's an experience I wouldn't recommend to anyone. It also meant I would have to wear a protective mask in the next match. From what I'd heard from other players, that wasn't going to be fun. It wasn't. It was something you especially don't want to have to do for the first time in a must-win game in the World Cup.

To compound the issue, my broken nose became part of a circus.

There was never any doubt that I was going to play in the next match against France. I woke up the next morning, met with the medical staff and then met with the mask-makers, who moulded my face. I was playing. Period.

I know what I need to do to prepare in a tournament, and my routine, developed over the years, is important to me. I'm not about to talk to the media on certain days, ever, but other days are fine.

The day after the game, our team's press relations people told me, "You're going to talk to the media." They wanted to parade me around.

I had a stupid little cast on my nose, and I said no.

"But people want to see you. They want to see your nose."

"I don't care what people want to see. We're still in the World Cup."

But Carolina and the PR people insisted that I go down to the hotel lobby and talk to the media. They also told me that during the buildup for our next game against France, we were going to try to create doubt as to whether I would be playing. That was Carolina's idea. It was all about getting a competitive edge. Her thinking was that our opponents would prepare differently if they weren't sure I'd be playing.

The truth is we do try to create little deceptions during tournaments. For instance, the media are only allowed in for the first ten or fifteen minutes of practice. Certain players may not practise for those first fifteen minutes, and then, as soon as the media leave, they're on the field. You do anything you can to create any type of question for the opponent.

But this was blown way out of proportion. The next thing I knew they had me riding a bike around the outside of the field instead of practising, with the media watching and trying to figure out what was going on. Did anyone care that I might need to be ready for a World Cup game? That I might want to practise with my mask on, because I needed to get used to it?

Our strength and conditioning guy, Mario, was the one who came up with the bike idea. "We don't want you running yet," he said. "Give your nose a day or two to set a little bit before you start bouncing up and down and running."

I've broken my nose since, and I understand that what he said made sense, to a point. But really? Riding a BMX bike around a practice field? Couldn't I just go to a gym and ride a stationary bike instead?

The answer was no, because Carolina was staging the whole production for the media.

Even my teammates didn't know exactly what was going on. They asked me a bunch of times whether I was going to be playing.

"Guys," I said, "of course, I'm playing."

My nose, and the whole media charade, wasn't the only issue.

We had five days to prepare between our first game against Germany and our second game against France. During that stretch we had precisely one team meeting.

We players were upset that we had lost to Germany, but thought it was a decent result. We believed we could take that game as a starting point and get better as the tournament went along.

But our staff didn't see the game as a respectable loss we could learn from. Instead, they were angry and frustrated with us over losing, and they couldn't move on, which created extra stress within the team—the players were now worried about making our own staff mad. Looking back, I think many of us had always been a little afraid of setting the coach and her staff off, but the pressures of the World Cup really heightened that fear. Not only weren't we preparing properly for the next game, but our coaching staff was looking backwards. Not only did they seem to underestimate the French team, but they also disregarded the fact that a win against them meant we still could do well in our group.

It was at that point that Carolina decided to use the World Cup stage as an opportunity to vent her concerns and frustrations with the CSA in the media. Our coaches have always had issues with the CSA; 99.9 percent of the time they conduct those fights behind closed doors. Carolina, who was always playing an angle, decided this was the moment to go public.

For one, she brought up the idea that we were wearing men's-cut jerseys, saying that the CSA hadn't even cared about the team enough to get us proper women's jerseys. It was the strangest thing—we had a team meeting about jerseys in the middle of the World Cup. I remember Carolina saying that she wasn't sure she could continue as our coach because of constantly having to fight with the CSA.

At one point, Rhian stuck her hand up and asked, "So are you quitting right now? In the middle of the World Cup?"

She wasn't quitting yet, but the whole time she was acting out her agenda, she wasn't doing anything to get us ready to play France.

I walked out onto the field for the France match angry because I had to wear the mask. You don't look down at the ball while you're dribbling, but you can still see it. You don't realize how much you use your peripheral vision while playing soccer until you can't use it. I couldn't see properly, and I hated the mask.

We all had done the math in our head, the way you always do in a tournament. All we had to do was not *lose* this game. With a draw, and then a win over Nigeria in our last group game, we'd probably still get through. The staff kept telling us not to worry, that we had this, that we could handle France.

But then the game started and, man, did we not have it.

France played out of their minds that day. I give them so much credit. It felt like everything they did wound up in the back of our net. Their play was crisp and clean. Since then, they have come to be regarded as one of the best teams in the world, and I think of that game as their coming-out party.

Unfortunately, it was against us.

It was clear that we were outmatched, especially when we fell behind 2–0. There are games when you're down 2–0 and you think, *We're in this. We just need one.* Then there are games when you're down 2–0 and you think, *Oh God, this is going to get ugly.*

This game was the ugly kind.

I don't remember Carolina or anyone else saying anything to us at halftime. I just remember our disappointment in ourselves, and our sadness because we knew this World Cup dream was over.

Playing for your country can be so rewarding. But when you fail on the grandest stage, you feel like you have let the country down, let down all the people who have supported you. You think about the teammates who are sitting on the bench and would do anything just to be in the game, or the ones who were cut right before the tournament, only to see the team go out there and lay an egg.

To make matters worse, right at the end of the game someone squared the ball off my face. The mask protected my nose, but it cut my eye. I was bleeding, we had lost 4–0, and our World Cup was over.

That's when you start thinking, *Why in the hell are we doing this? What is the point?*

I'm not sure it was the worst moment of my career; I've had a few doozies. But it was right up there.

Afterwards, there were a lot of tears. A *lot* of tears. There was a lot of time spent consoling teammates.

After the France game, we still had another game to play and six more days to spend mulling over our tournament, but we only saw our staff twice. They no longer came to meals. I'm not joking. They purposely went to lunch an hour later than we did and to dinner an hour earlier so they wouldn't run into us. It was so depressing. It was clear that they thought the failure was all ours. They didn't call a single meeting to prepare for our last game against Nigeria. We saw the coaches and staff only at practice, and otherwise felt very much like we were on our own.

I remember feeling such relief when I talked to my professional team back in the States. Here we were preparing for our third game in the World Cup, and I was figuring out when I needed to fly home to join my club.

The players decided to run our own meeting to watch film of Nigeria's games. Even though we were already out of the running, we were still playing in a World Cup. If the staff wasn't going to do it, we would do it ourselves.

But in that final match, it was clear that Nigeria was out there fighting. We weren't. We tried to muster up the energy, but we were done, all of us just waiting to go home.

Nigeria beat Canada 1–0. It was a big moment for them.

It also meant that we had finished dead last in the World Cup.

The end of a tournament is always weird, whether it ends in success or failure.

You've spent all this time with your teammates. You've worked so hard, and whether you've won or lost, you've put in the blood and the sweat and the tears. And then on the final night, you have dinner with the team, head off to bed and the next morning everyone's gone.

Some of the players flew home from Germany right away. I had some friends in town who had come to watch the matches, so I spent time with them. Then Rhian, Karina, Diana and I went to Prague for a couple of days. We watched one of the World Cup games on television there and it was just the worst feeling ever. It was so painful, and all of us were thinking that we could have been there.

I honestly had no idea about the future. I remember talking with my teammates in Prague and all of us were wondering what the point was anymore. *Why are we doing this? Is it worth it?*

We had sacrificed so much time and energy. We had missed big events in our family's lives. And for what? We were angry at everyone and everything. And the CSA didn't seem to care what had happened to us. As much as her timing was off, big time, Carolina's complaints about the CSA were legitimate. We were a team that regularly qualified for World Cups and the Olympics and we were still having to battle for the most basic support. Aside from some attention from the media, it seemed like soccer in Canada was going nowhere.

I remember asking myself whether I really wanted to be a part of another cycle of this. There were Olympics coming up in London the following year, but who the heck was going to be our coach? Not Carolina, that's for sure.

It was awful all around, but somehow, I never got to the point where I said, "I'm done."

I did learn something from that experience, though. A coach and a staff don't make a team. In the deepest, darkest place, when you've just finished dead last at a World Cup, you learn what your passion is. It took a while to rediscover it, but there was a reason why I started playing soccer when I was four. It truly was for the love of the game. I think as an athlete I could have done well in multiple sports. But I chose a team sport, and in moments of defeat such as the one after that World Cup, you realize why. You fight as a team. You win as a team. And you lose as a team.

You also learn to trust your family and listen to what they have to say. When it comes right down to it, you realize most voices from the outside world don't matter. I knew that my family would always be there for me. I wasn't a soccer player to them. I was their daughter or sister or niece or cousin or aunt. I was me.

If we had listened to the critics and the peanut gallery after the 2011 World Cup, I think it would have destroyed all of us. My family were the ones who reminded me that I had so much to be proud of, that playing soccer at this level was what I had always wanted and what I and the other women on our team had fought for.

At my first World Cup in 2003, we finished fourth and not too many people at home really cared. Now, even though the tournament had been a disaster, people cared. We had at least changed that about soccer in Canada.

9

EARNING MY DOCTORATE IN SOCCER

I'm the type that, if things go poorly in a match or a tournament, I want to go back and play as soon as possible.

I was fortunate that I was playing for the Flash, so I could head back to my pro team in Buffalo after the World Cup and finish the season. It was an escape. The team was stacked with talent, and it was fun to play without the stress of a World Cup. It allowed me to be in denial for a little bit, to focus on other things.

We won the Women's Professional Soccer championship at the end of August—and then the league folded. That was heartbreaking. There goes another one. It was the dream of so many of us to play professionally, and to have another women's pro league go under felt like crap.

Obviously, Carolina was done as Canada's head coach. Right after the pro season ended, Peter Montopoli from the CSA called to tell me that John Herdman was being hired as her replacement. The first camp with him was a couple of weeks away.

I knew John from his days coaching the New Zealand national women's team. The players laugh about it now, but until he became our guy, we thought of him as that annoying little man on the sideline wearing an earpiece.

I told Peter that I needed a break—I wasn't ready to get back with the national team just yet. The pro season had just ended, and the last thing I wanted was to go straight into a camp. So I didn't go.

Instead, I hit the road, driving from Buffalo to Portland with a friend. We stopped in Cedar Point, Ohio, for the roller coasters, and at Yellowstone National Park and a bunch of other places along the way. By the time I got home, I hadn't had to think about soccer for almost three weeks.

But there was one moment that brought me back to the game. During that first camp with John, Canada had played a friendly against the US. As I watched it on television, I felt the pang of not being there. Playing the US is always the contest that gets you going. I'd also been hearing from teammates that this new coach was incredible.

You could already see the difference John had made with the team. Tanc had sliced her head open in that match and was playing with a bandage wrapped around her forehead. Then she scored and the first thing she did was run to John.

For Tanc, that was saying something significant.

And that's when I knew it was time to bring it on again. Not to mention that for the moment, with my pro league folded, I had nowhere else to play soccer.

I was back with the national team for John's second camp, which was designed to prepare us for the Pan American Games that fall in Guadalajara, Mexico. I will always remember that tournament as the birth of the unstoppable force that is Desiree Scott. John played her at the six—the defensive midfielder. It was her first time playing the position, and she has never given it up. She was new to the team at the time, and she just came in and owned it.

What else do I remember about Guadalajara?

They hadn't quite finished building the athletes' village when the games began. There were six or eight people per apartment, and ours sort of flooded. I guess that's the Pan Am Games for you—kind of the budget Olympics.

But more importantly, that competition was the first time any Canadian national soccer team won gold. And to do it, we beat the defending champion, Brazil, with Marta in the lineup. Late in the game, Brazil was up 1–0, and Diana Matheson hit a corner. I got my head on it, and we scored to tie the game, and then we won in a shootout. Karina LeBlanc just stood on her head to block the Brazilian shooters. Man, we've produced some good goalkeepers over the years.

We had won bronze at the previous Pan Ams in Rio, so moving up and winning gold in our first tournament playing under John was a big deal. It's an unbelievable feeling to stand on the top of the podium as you listen to your national anthem play. I remember joking to the press that the medal was a present for my mom, who'd just had her birthday a couple days earlier. Also, it was a pretty great start for a new coach. Must have reassured him he'd made the right move.

The plan was to reassemble for a camp in Los Angeles late in the year to get us ready for the CONCACAF Olympic qualifying tournament. And then, so long as we qualified, and with no North American professional league to play in, we would have a long residency in Vancouver leading up to the 2012 London Games.

John Herdman is the best coach I've ever had, hands down. He is life-changing.

Let me edit that slightly. I had Clive Charles in college, but I only had him for two years before he passed away, and he was sick almost the entire time. So, let me say again that John is the best, but with an asterisk in my heart for Clive.

John always says that every team he puts out will be the most prepared team on the field. The first time I heard him say that I kind of rolled my eyes, but he was telling the truth. Every single game under him, we knew we were more prepared than our opponent. We knew exactly what they were going to do and how we were going to exploit it and the three different formations we were going to play to do it.

John prided himself in giving a doctorate in soccer to all his players—that's exactly how he said it. I had been playing at a high level for years, but he taught me the sport in a way that I had never been exposed to before. All the analysis, all the data, all the GPS tracking, all the small, intricate details of your game. It's not just counting goals; it's the turning, dribbling, crosses, shots and final acts. John's staff gathered all the information that told you exactly where you were as a player. Seeing the data on me for the first time was just mind-blowing.

I think John worked from 5 a.m. to midnight every day. I still don't really understand how he functions. On top of that intense work ethic, he has the unique ability to motivate and galvanize a team. He is a great talker. If he ever decided to do it for a living, he'd be the best motivational speaker in the world.

John has always said that all he needed to do in 2012 was help us rediscover our passion—we were already built for success because of what we'd experienced in 2011. He just needed to help us fall in love with the game again and remember how to have fun.

Both as a team and as individual players, we instantaneously bought into what John was telling us, because we were so thirsty and in need of something new. We did deep dives as a group. We held three-hour-long meetings, going around the group with each of us sharing and being honest and open. We talked about finding our "whys": *Why do I play? Why am I here?* John knew that he had to let us discover that for ourselves, but he made sure we had the opportunity to do so. He is all about individuals being vulnerable in front of each other and sharing emotions. If you can do that in a meeting room, you'll do anything for each other on the field.

I'll admit it was hard for me. I'm super close with my teammates, because I know them and they know me—knowledge developed over years of association in intense situations. But I didn't know John. So there I was being vulnerable in front of a new coach and a staff, feeling really uncomfortable. But I was willing to dive in because I trusted my teammates, who all told me that John was the real deal.

Outside of soccer, we were a diverse group in a lot of ways. But John can connect with almost anyone. His attitude is, "I want to connect with the heart first, and if I can't win over your heart then I shouldn't be your coach." He has this unique ability to get to your core.

He is also brutally honest in an amazing way. With him as our coach, we all had to learn how to be honest with each other and with the whole team. We'd be talking in meetings and John would say, "That's fluff. Be more specific. No one's going to respond to that. Say how you really feel." Some meetings I walked out at the end and realized that we hadn't talked about soccer at all. What the heck? It was like two hours of being in therapy.

John believed in us, and we needed to hear that. From day one, he talked about reaching the podium at the London Olympic Games.

I remember thinking, *Dude, those are in seven months. What are you talking about?* But it was pretty cool to hear someone say out loud that he actually thought we could do it. Not just any someone, but our coach.

Everyone sees the product John puts out on the field: you can notice a night-and-day change in teams pre-John and post-John. You saw it with us and you're seeing it now with the Canadian men's national team.

But what you don't see is how much he cares about his players. I don't know if it's the same with the men, but with the women, he dove into our lives. When my father died (which I'll say a little more about later), his wife helped my brother and me arrange his funeral, and John spoke at the service. When he's in your corner he's in your corner forever. There are so many things that are more important than what you do on the soccer field. John truly wants you to grow and develop as a person, just as my other best coach did.

I remember him once telling Karina that if her legacy was just that she had been a soccer player for Canada, he'd failed her. He sees the potential in people and does his best to get it out.

He helped us define bigger goals than winning a soccer game or winning a tournament, and we rallied around them. For London, we wanted to inspire a generation and see the flag rise. That's what drove us every day. It drove our training; it drove how we decided what to eat and not eat. We bought in completely. We had never had that kind of focus before.

He showed us we were capable of so much more and helped us believe it. What had happened at the World Cup in Germany—whether it was the coach, whether it was us, whether we were unlucky, whether we just had a crap tournament—wasn't going to define us.

There was a very, very strong group of women on that team, and we weren't okay with what had happened in 2011. Karina, Rhian, Diana, Tanc—there was no way that disastrous World Cup was going to be their legacy. Or mine.

The Olympic qualifying was held in Vancouver. Even when it's happening in your own hometown, that tournament is nerve-racking. As I've mentioned, it pretty much comes down to one game to decide whether you make it or not. In 2012, we knew that game would be the semi-final against Mexico. I had been down that road before. We'd lost to them in 2004, which kept us from qualifying for the Athens Games.

But right from the start of the tournament, you could see everything that we had worked on with John coming together on the field. We've never played the most beautiful style of soccer. It's not who our team is and it's not what we're built on. But individual players were coming into their own because John had given them that confidence— Christina Julien and Tanc and Brit Timko and so many others. I remember thinking, *We could be lethal if we keep playing like this.*

We were *back*. The crowds were amazing. And we were smiling again, playing in front of our friends and family.

I hadn't had the chance to play at home a ton. Sharing that experience with my family was really special. It was the first time my older niece, five at the time, got to go on the field. She started playing youth soccer after that, and she was so confused: she thought all games were supposed to be at BC Place.

We cruised through the group stage, winning all three games. Then we beat Mexico 3–1 in the semifinal to lock up our Olympic berth. The crowd went crazy, and there was a big celebration on the field.

The final in a qualifying tournament is a bonus. There's nothing on the line except pride. We played the United States again, and in a tournament like that the Americans' depth just kills everyone else. They could field two completely different rosters and one would be the best team in the world and the other would be the second-best team in the world. A Canada or Mexico, playing our sixth game in two weeks, just can't compete.

We knew we were up against long odds. And it's a good thing the game didn't matter to our Olympic chances, because the US beat us 4–0.

I could write a whole book about what it's like to play against the Americans. They're the number-one team in the world for a reason. To start with, they're frickin' good, and they know exactly how good they are, which can be annoying. They have what seems like unlimited resources and an unlimited talent pool, a never-ending pipeline of world-class players.

Even though they came into BC Place and killed us in that match, we still knew we were on the right path. But we also knew that we still had a lot of work to do to get up to their level.

It's hard for me to say what I'm about to say, because I've become good friends with a lot of the US players. The women's soccer world is so small. And, as I've said, I respect the way American players have led the fight for equality and for equal pay and for professional leagues.

But, man, something happens when they put on that US jersey and we put on our Canadian jersey.

For the longest time we were the little sister. They were always bigger, they always had more, and we were always trying to grasp and claw just to get to their level.

But they have an attitude, often the case with very successful teams, that is just so obnoxious. You have to respect what they put into every game, but they act like every game is a World Cup final. To constantly lose to them—and in our region, CONCACAF, it always comes down to them—is hard. I'm sure if Germany or France were in our region, we'd be feeling similarly about them, too. But for us, it's always the US.

In a way they are what we want to become—except in a friendlier, Canadian kind of way.

I am not close with Abby Wambach, who was the captain of that American team. It has nothing to do with me not liking her or her not liking me. It's just that our paths have rarely crossed. We have never played on the same professional team. I don't know her that well. I do have a lot of respect for her. She's obviously an incredible goal scorer and she's one of the few players that I've played against who, like Brazil's Marta, can single-handedly will a team to win.

And, as annoying as it is, she will do anything to help her team. Whether that's getting in a ref's ear or anything else, it's because Abby wants so badly to win, and I respect that. But the two of us go about our work a little differently.

When we play against each other, there isn't a lot of trash talk. You see that kind of thing more in some of the male sports, but it's not really there in the women's game, where so many of us play professionally with and against each other. There's some talk on the field, but it's more because you're friends. For instance, Becky Sauerbrunn is my teammate on the Portland Thorns. When I'm up against her when she's playing for the US, I might say something to her, but it's out of fun because we're also teammates. It's not the in-your-face stuff you see on TV.

Every once in a while, people do have something unflattering to say. I've been called an "old hag" on the field. That's my personal favourite so far in my career.

But most of the on-field talk is directed at the refs. Naturally, everything is the refs' fault.

A team residency is awful and amazing all at once. It's like four months of pre-season in a row, which is very hard and draining and exhausting. But the amount of work you can get done, especially with a new coach, is so helpful.

John is all about the details, and spending that time with him before London allowed us to nit-pick the little things. It set us apart from some of the other teams that were just coming together during the FIFA international playing windows. In Europe, national teams don't do residencies because of the demands made on the players by their pro teams. Every day we had together was an advantage for us, and we knew it. Plus, living in downtown Vancouver was a blast.

I'm not going to lie—we really believed we'd get to the podium in London. We were convinced we would do it even when no one else thought it was possible. Technically and tactically, we were going to be the most prepared team at the Olympics, hands down. When the draw came out and we knew who our opponents were going to be, we spent a week focusing on each team that we were going to play. John's level of attention to detail is just insane.

We played the Americans in Utah in a friendly at the end of June, just before we headed to Europe. In a lot of ways, it was a typical Canada-US game. Erin was great in goal. Tanc scored to tie it 1–1 and went into her celebration routine. Then the Americans scored late and ended up winning 2–1. It was evident to all of us that we'd made progress since the qualifiers. But, again, it was one of those games where we were waiting for the US to score the winning goal. That's kind of how it went with them against us. They always seemed to find a way to win.

I don't really remember how I felt after that match, but I'm sure I was pissed. Maybe days later you look back and think it's all right—if they're the best team in the world we're still in a good spot. But knowing me and knowing the team, the feeling would have been anger and disappointment and frustration. Moral victories are not that great in sport. They don't do much for you.

10

"I'M NOT LEAVING WITHOUT A MEDAL. SO, LET'S GO."

John likes to take his teams away somewhere to train before a big competition. Ahead of London we had a pre-tournament camp in the Alps—in Crans-Montana, Switzerland, where we lived in a little ski chalet. It was amazing. Secluded in this beautiful place with very little outside contact, we focused on the goal of getting onto the podium and seeing the flag rise and inspiring a generation.

Robyn Gayle and Mel Booth were roommates, and they had a countdown on the mirror in their room of how many days were left until we kicked off. It was frightening how ready that group was. It was such a good bonding trip.

There was a little mini tournament in preparation for the Olympics. New Zealand and Brazil were there. We destroyed New Zealand. We were flying on the pitch that day. And then we played Brazil. We tied the game late, but then Marta took the ball from the kickoff after our tying goal and dribbled through our whole team and scored the winner.

We were all right, but that was a bit of a wake-up call.

Still, we knew that our 2012 team was built for the moment. John had it all down to a science, just like he had everything down to a science. He calculated the number of caps he thought we needed to win—balancing internationally experienced players and ones new to that stage, and mixing veterans with younger athletes who had already played with the team and new ones with no experience at the national level.

We had young players like Jonelle Filigno, Kaylyn Kyle and Chelsea Stewart. And older players, like me and Erin McLeod, who were the veterans of the group. I remember what it was like for me as a sixteen-year-old to join the national team, and how intimidated I was by veterans like Charmaine Hooper. But the young ones of this roster didn't seem all that scared of me.

The hard part for me in connecting with new teammates is that I am very shy. It's not my natural behaviour to be outgoing until I really get to know you. It's not that I want to be standoffish, but I know I can seem that way. A Desi Scott or an Erin McLeod is out there immediately welcoming new players, whereas I'm just not built that way. It's a work in progress for me to step out of my comfort zone. And even in my comfort zone, I'm usually a quiet person.

I remember for one of Jessie Fleming's first camps they thought it would be great for us to be roommates. Honestly, it was the worst nightmare for both of us, because we're both shy, so there wasn't much talking in that room. I could tell that she was at least a little uncomfortable. I've been there. It's the worst.

On that London team, the pieces and personalities just seemed to fit together perfectly.

Let's start with Tanc—Melissa Tancredi—my strike buddy. There's no one I'd rather have on my team than her. I'm not comparing her personality to Abby Wambach's, but in terms of competitiveness and doing anything to help the team win, that's who she's most like. She's one of the best teammates you can have, given that she's a great competitor but also a bit of a clown in the locker room. Tanc is always there to bring out the energy.

She's also a clutch, big-game performer, unstoppable when it matters most. And after London, she's the one that I give credit to for taking Jessie Fleming under her wing and helping her blossom. Tanc was one hundred percent responsible for Jessie coming out of her shell—and, of course, if you're reading this, you know what happened in Tokyo.

Tanc became a chiropractor after she retired as a player in 2017. She'd managed to do her doctorate while she was still playing, which is just unbelievable. And now she's part of the team's medical staff.

While we're on the subject of London, I have to talk about Desi Scott. The Pan Ams in 2011 were her arrival;

by the time we got to London, she was the best defensive midfielder in the world. Back then she was quieter than she is now, but she was already a rock, another player who would sacrifice anything to help the team win. She comes out of games with bruises and cuts everywhere. There's a reason why we all call her "The Destroyer"— she's absolutely fearless. She's one of the strongest people I've ever met, and, as I've gotten to know her, I've come to realize that she is also one of the kindest and most gentle souls around. Off the field she's a softie. On the field she's the complete opposite.

Erin McLeod and I are the last two survivors who played the U19 tournament in Edmonton. We've literally grown up together. Well, I don't know how much we've grown up, but at least we've aged together.

She is the most unlucky person when it comes to injuries, which breaks my heart. It seemed like every time she reached the top of her game—and by that I mean the best goalkeeper in the world—she'd get hurt. In London she was vitally important for us during the whole tournament, but especially in the game against France. I don't want to know what the score would have been if we hadn't had Erin. And her composure, how calm she is—I don't know how she does it. I know people think that goalkeepers are all weird—they play a position where you regularly get the ball booted off your face. And because of that unique job, they also train on their own and have separate gym sessions. But Erin is surprisingly normal.

And now she's taken on a role within the NWSL and with the Players Association, fighting for equality, fighting for equal pay and equal rights. It's an inspiration to all of us.

Robyn Gayle is just the best human being ever. During the London Olympics, she hurt her hamstring in the first game and didn't think she'd be able to play, so she gave her jersey to Mel Booth, her roommate, who was an alternate on the team. It was like the scene in the movie *Rudy*, where each of Rudy's Notre Dame teammates hands in their jersey so he'll be given the opportunity, at last, to play a game in their place. There was a chance Robyn could come back for the knockout round, but she didn't want to take up a roster spot for the next four games if she couldn't play. That selflessness tells you everything about her.

Now she's working for the CSA as the mental and cultural manager for both the women's and men's national teams. That role is her in a nutshell. She has the ability to balance a sense of a team alongside a sense of each individual. She was like that when she was playing, and now it's her job.

The women's team loves her. At first, I did wonder if the men's team was going to buy into her role, but I've heard nothing but wonderful things about her from them. When the men played that World Cup qualifying match in Edmonton against Mexico in November 2021, I was watching on television. After Canada won, all the players celebrated on the field and then got into a bit of a fight with some of the Mexican team. Robyn was right there in the middle of it, trying to do her job: mental and cultural manager, for sure. I remember texting her and saying, "What are you doing? You don't know how to throw a punch."

I've already made the point that athletes who have had good coaching tend to stay on in the sport after they are through playing. Rhian Wilkinson pointed out to me that 95 percent of the players on our 2012 Olympic team have stayed in the game one way or another, whether it's playing or coaching or broadcasting or working on a medical staff. That's another tribute to John, and how he helped us fall in love with the game again. Just look at how many of his players are still involved.

Rhian is now my coach with the Portland Thorns. Karina LeBlanc is our general manager, and before that she worked for CONCACAF and in sports broadcasting. I already mentioned that Robyn is involved with both the men's and women's national teams. Tanc is on the medical staff. And on and on it goes.

That's John Herdman's legacy. And his contribution to Canadian soccer isn't done yet.

The women's Olympic soccer tournament always begins before the rest of the competitions, which is why we never march in the opening ceremonies. And in London, unless we made it to the gold medal final in Wembley Stadium, none of our matches would be in the city, so we weren't going to spend much time in the main Olympic Village either. John made a point of getting us to England early so that we could at least experience the village.

After we landed in London, we got on our bus and it immediately got lost. We had been driving for forty-five minutes before we noticed that we were passing the airport again. You'd think the driver might have figured out the route from the airport to the Olympic Village in advance. But other than that, the experience was great. We checked into the village and stayed in the Canada building for a couple of days. We got our team gear, which is always fun, as well as an important first taste of the Olympics.

We were like tourists on crack, trying to cram in as much as we could. The Olympic Village has unique things to offer. You've got to hit up the store, because everyone back home wants souvenirs. The experience of the food hall is just wild. There are so many people of so many different nationalities, and so many different cuisines on offer (plus, for some reason, always McDonald's). For a lot of us, it was our first time in London. We went to see the Changing of the Guard, we rode the London Eye, we went to London Bridge. We saw a performance of *The Lion King* in the West End. That was all in one day. We took the tube everywhere and just soaked it all in. Afterwards, we needed a vacation from our day of vacation.

But that was pretty much it for London. We spent most of the rest of the Games in Coventry—we joked that it was really the Coventry Olympics. Our first two games were there, our quarterfinal game was there, and the bronze medal match was there.

We watched the opening ceremonies on television in our hotel in Coventry. The organizers did try to make the place a little like the athletes' village. Some of the men's soccer teams were staying there, too, and the Olympic Committee set up a viewing party for us. We marched in and pretended we were part of it. Cheesy, but fun.

I always get anxious the night before our first match and tend not to sleep well. I have full trust in our team—it's just tournament nerves. There's nothing that makes it easier: not confidence, not experience, nothing. But along with the rest of the team, I felt a sense of belief and purpose. A sense of being prepared. A sense of being ready. I knew we'd put in the work and that there was nothing we'd left undone. There was a sense of togetherness on our team. Our teams had always been close, but this particular group felt different in terms of how connected we were. That core had been together for a long time. We had the coach, we had the prep. It was time to play, hoping that what we did in the buildup was right.

Our first match was with Japan. They were an incredible test for us right out of the gate; they were that good.

But it was go-time, and goal one was to get out of the group. Olympics, torturous in qualification rounds, are a little less stressful than some tournaments, because three teams advance out of your initial group of four (unless you're the worst third-place team in the groups round).

John had this whole concept about "growing" into a tournament. There have been teams that just steamroll the whole thing and win everything. But winning teams usually face some adversity along the way. They build over the course of the competition. Teams that get better along the way are usually the ones that are successful.

So when we lost to Japan in the opener, we weren't overly devastated. They're a great team. When you line up against them, you think, *We're going to dominate these guys*, because they're smaller-statured and don't look physically imposing at all. But you hardly ever touch the ball because they're so technically sound and gifted and organized. They take such pride in always having the ball. In set pieces, where play restarts after a foul or a ball going out of play, and you have the ball, you can get the best of them because you can take advantage of your height. But in the run of play, it's hard to beat them.

John had us set up to defend well and hit them on the counter, which we did. And since our goal wasn't to win the first game at all costs, losing didn't really change the game plan. After the match was over, we leaned into what we called our "Dory" concept. That's Dory, the character from the movie *Finding Nemo*. If you've seen the movie, you know that when something happens to Dory, she immediately forgets it. That became a team thing. Win or lose in the Olympics, you have to get over it really fast because you've got another game in forty-eight hours.

So we'd lost. Forget about it and move on. It was the same thing on the field. Someone made a mistake or even two—snap out of it, forget it, let's go.

We had nailed quick-turnaround tournaments like this in the past and had become a fine-tuned machine. Every player had their individual routines for recovery—treatment, massage, ice. Everyone knew what they had to do to be ready for the next game. We also knew that we did have to win our second game, against South Africa, by at least a couple of goals; goal differentials can be critical when it comes to a third-place team going through. And the last game, against Sweden, was going to be a big one.

We headed into the South Africa match with so much confidence. With John's heavy concentration on fielding the most-prepared team, we figured we were going to be more ready than they were. That turned out to be true: we were more ready than they were and we knew exactly how to exploit their weaknesses.

We won 3–0. I scored a couple of goals and was feeling great about my game. I was on fire.

Sophie Schmidt was my roommate during that tournament, and both of us felt a similar sense of confidence in ourselves and the team. We were at the peak of our careers. We knew we could have a huge impact. It's a very powerful thing when you know you can be the difference in any game, let alone in an Olympic match.

Sometimes with tournaments you're just unlucky, or you're not heading in healthy. I think our team was as physically fit as it had ever been, thanks to the residency camp. Our strength and conditioning coach worked us into the ground, in a healthy way. Knowing you're fit gives you so much faith, and then you add a coach who knows how to get the best out of you, not only individually but as a team. It's funny what confidence can do.

Believe it or not, I had felt the same way heading into the World Cup in 2011. One thing Carolina did for me was give me a lot of confidence as a player. But John was able to build confidence team-wide. Everybody had bought in. Everybody knew their role. Everyone was in the right place.

We had injuries throughout the course of the tournament, which is always hard, but when that happened in London, it was next person up.

Our third game, against Sweden, was a good time.

It was held in Newcastle, John Herdman's hometown, at St. James' Park, the famous stadium where Newcastle United plays. When we walked into the park the day before the game, I'd never seen John so proud. We knew that his dream job was coaching Newcastle United (he's not shy about telling you that), and he pointed out where he'd sat in the stands as a kid. We all could tell that it meant a lot to him to be coaching us there in an Olympic Games.

Newcastle's big local rival is Sunderland. They wear red. And, obviously, Canada wears red. Newcastle's colours are black and white. As a team we decided that we were going to wear black warm-up tops and black jackets to win over the fans, and as a show of support for John. That went over great.

And then the game started, and before you could blink it was 2–0 Sweden.

After their second goal I remember thinking, *Guys, if we lose 6–0 or something like that, we're going to be out of the tournament because of goal differential.* In a tournament, you know where you need to be, and a massive defeat to Sweden wasn't going to do it for us. I started to have flashbacks to the terrible game against France in the 2011 World Cup.

But our team was different now. We rallied, and we fought, and we did it the Canadian way, scrapping and clawing. When Tanc scored before the end of the first half, the game changed. We dominated the rest of the way. Tanc scored again late—remember I said she was always a clutch player? All of us ran to the sideline in celebration.

The score was tied, and based on that result we knew we'd be through to the next round. But the difference between a tie and a win would determine which team we played in the quarterfinals. In the middle of celebrating Tanc's second goal, John was yelling at us: "What do you guys want to do? Do you want to go for the win?"

He already knew the answer. We wanted to play for the win.

We didn't get it. The game ended in a 2–2 tie, which meant we finished third in our group. We would have to wait for the result of the Great Britain and Brazil match to find out who we were playing—we'd get the winner.

All of us watched that game in the lobby of our hotel in Newcastle, with the friends and family who were in town. Great Britain won, which surprised just about everyone. That meant we were going up against the home team in our first knockout game at the Olympics.

Heck, yeah. Home country? Home crowd? Let's go!

England is a really good team. Kelly Smith is one of the greatest female players ever. And at the Olympics, they play as Great Britain, which means they can also add the best players from Scotland, Wales and Northern Ireland.

Even so, I don't remember being super nervous heading into that game. I knew we could beat them. That's what John had instilled in us. We took the bus back to Coventry the next day, and all the players had their laptops out studying Team GB. A couple of us had a meeting with John and showed him things we had noticed, spaces we could expose. His players were going to *him* with ideas— that's how into it we were. We knew Great Britain had certain weaknesses, and we developed a plan to exploit them.

Then, on the day of the match, the rosters came out and we found out that Kelly Smith was out with a charley horse. We decided that meant they weren't taking us seriously. You don't miss a game in the Olympics because of a charley horse.

Obviously, we didn't know the whole story, and injuries do happen. But whether or not what we were thinking was right, we used it for motivation. *You're going to be injured for our game? Well, enjoy your holiday.* Any time you can create a little edge for yourself in a contest like that, you do it. It doesn't have to be true, just as long as your brain believes it.

We played well. I remember Jonelle scored off a corner. After the game, Simon Eaddy, who was our goalkeeper coach and also worked on our set plays, showed us a video clip of the goal from British television.

The announcers were analyzing it—talking about how smart it was, how brilliantly we had done. The ball was kind of played on the ground and Jonelle came around and hammered it top corner. An unbelievable strike!

We all died laughing, because Sophie had taken the corner and shanked it. It was not our play at all. The idea was something we had practised on the training ground, but the execution wasn't what we'd hope for. It was so funny that the announcers thought we were soccer geniuses.

After that I scored on a free kick. I remember running to the bench to celebrate, and Karina wound up with stud marks down her leg because I slid into her.

We were actually a bunch of goofballs.

Then we just held on—and man, that stadium got quiet.

It was nice to play with a lead. It was still stressful, but it's a lot easier being up 2–0 than to be tied heading into the last ten minutes.

John had called it: we *had* grown through the tournament. You could see it. We had faced adversity and we hadn't won every game, but we were coming together at the right time. That was our whole goal. Sure, it would be great to win every game 6–0, but so long as we could improve in every game, we could get to the podium.

We also knew who we were up against next.

Going to Old Trafford to play the Americans. This was going to be fun . . .

To that point, I had only beaten the United States twice in my career. The first time was when I was sixteen, during my first year on the national team. The Americans had just won the 1999 World Cup and we beat them 3–1. I scored in that game. I remember thinking, *Oh my God, we just beat the Americans—it can be done.* We'd also beaten them in an Algarve Cup. Karina LeBlanc was part of that. We were the only two players on the 2012 Olympic team who knew what it felt like to beat the United States.

I hadn't anticipated it would take quite so long to have that experience for a third time.

But I also had never been on a Canadian team that was where we were at that moment. I knew that it was at least going to be a fight. If they were going to beat us, they were going to do it with blood coming down their faces.

The US always plays the same way, because they know they're better at it than anyone else. In their minds, no matter what you do, you're not going to stop them. (The only time I've ever seen them change tactics against us was in

Tokyo, when they went to a different formation. I guess that showed we had earned their respect, a little bit.)

I remember the bus ride to Old Trafford very vividly. No surprise, but I'm a massive soccer fan, a huge English Premier League (EPL) fan, and specifically a fan of Liverpool Football Club. The rest of my family are all Manchester United supporters. I'm not sure how that happened. I think I went rogue.

It was the weirdest pre-big-match bus ride I have ever taken, because I remember not really thinking about the game at all. I was more focused on trying to spot Old Trafford out the window. It was the one stadium we didn't visit the day before the game. We were fried after the trip from Coventry to Manchester, and the staff decided it was more important for us to recover and rest than to train. "It's just a soccer field," they told us. "You'll see it when we get there."

I have a routine on game days. I go to the locker room first. I get changed. Then I head out onto the field because I need to see it day-of, even if I've seen it the day before.

When we got to Old Trafford, there was a big drama happening. We were technically the home team, but the US had shown up early and claimed the home locker room. We were stuck in a locker room that was—seriously—a closet. Here we were in this immaculate stadium, and the visitors' locker room was trash. It was unbelievable. There are nicer locker rooms just about everywhere else I've played.

The staff did a good job of not really letting us become aware of what was happening, though some of us did keep asking, "Hey, aren't we supposed to be the home team?"

Then I went out on the field for the first time. I remember telling myself, *You have two minutes. Take it in, don't think about the game, just take in Old Trafford.*

Everyone else was out there too, walking around the grass and taking selfies. Robyn Gayle, who was injured, had somehow got an all-access pass, and she was running around all over the place, in the press box, everywhere, getting pictures. You wouldn't think we were about to play an Olympic semifinal.

I do better when I don't think about the game, so it was a nice escape for me. I've played in some other amazing stadiums, including the Maracanã in Rio de Janeiro. But for me, Old Trafford was the best. There are other places that probably have more history, but you see Old Trafford on TV every other weekend watching the EPL. It's just different, and it was amazing to be there myself.

Then we went back in and got dressed and came out for warm-ups. At that point, things got serious. All I could think was, *This is going to be a battle.*

The US thought they were going to roll in and just kill us. What they didn't know was that there was something different about us. We were there to win . . .

—

There are some games where it seems like everything clicks. You're not doing anything different, but everything seems to work. I think of the U19s back in Edmonton, when we played England. I scored five goals that day because, for some reason, everything worked.

You make the little flick pass. Half the time it goes to the opponent, and half the time you find Tanc. Other than the first one, even the goals against the Americans could have gone the other way. The two headers? Seven times out of ten those don't go in. You work on corners relentlessly in training, but to get everything right—the delivery, the picks—there are so many moving parts.

I don't know why that game worked out for me the way it did. I didn't do anything out of the norm. It was one of those days where everything just . . . clicked. I prepared no differently. I didn't train differently. I didn't suddenly become a better soccer player between the Great Britain game and the US match.

I just felt such a sense of calm, or at least the kind of calm you feel inside chaos. It was one of those games where you're in the zone and not thinking about anything. You don't hear the fans. You're not worried about the result. You're just playing.

A sports psychiatrist named Ceri Evans was working with the team at the time. Before us, he'd worked with the formidable New Zealand All Blacks. We spent hours and hours and hours and hours together talking about how to live in the moment on the field. I had never done that before, at least not to any extent. Ceri hooked up electrodes to measure my brainwaves, trying to teach me how to get into a calm and focused state so I could do that on the ready. I've been doing that kind of work ever since.

We also had our sports psychologist, Alex Hodgins, who has been with the team for at least eight years. A lot of players have fully bought into what he does. If you ask Jessie Fleming how she stays calm taking PKs, she'll say, "My work with Alex. Thanks to him I know how to get my brain to a calm place."

I know athletes say that when you're "in the zone" the game slows down around you. I think for me the challenge is to get to a place where I'm not thinking, just playing. I can only remember a half-dozen games where it's been completely like that.

I'm a forward—a goal scorer—so when people see me score three goals in a game, they would assume that's the impact on the game I'm aiming for. But that's not always the case. You can influence a game in a lot of ways, but obviously people pay the most attention to who scores.

When I scored my third goal, I ran to the bench to celebrate with everyone.

To this day, John says, "I don't know what was in your head. You looked like a crazy person. What got into you?" I have no idea. I think it was the effect of years and years of being beaten by them—not just being beaten, but having our team not even show up. We had previously played like we knew they were better, like we knew they were going to beat us. We would play not to lose, and if you do that, you never win.

This was one of the first times, maybe *the* first time, we were playing to win against the Americans. They still had their chances; they're the best team in the world for a reason. But we were going toe-to-toe and blow-to-blow with them, and it was so much fun. I get attention because I scored the goals, but the whole team played out of their skin. I'd never seen so many of our players have the game of their lives. Desiree, Tanc, Rhian. Jonelle Filigno ran herself into the ground.

I thought we were going to win all the way through the game, right up to the second the ref blew the whistle to end it. I had never seen our team play like that. We didn't lose the fight. We didn't lose the grit and battling spirit and connectedness that made us unique. But it was also the first time playing against the US where that wasn't all we had going for us.

It's been more than ten years, and I still have not watched that game. Because of the way it ended, I've never been able to bring myself to do it, and I never will. It would just be too depressing. I'd throw a chair through a window.

I've never seen a six-second call against a goalkeeper without any warning. I didn't count how long Erin had the ball in her hands, but if you watch the sport, goalkeepers often have the ball in their hands for a good twelve seconds. It happens all the time.

Until that call, I didn't have any real issue with the ref, though I remember Abby Wambach was working her constantly:

"Ref, six seconds."

"Ref, Ref, Ref, how much time are you gonna give her?"

"Ref, that's a handball."

Just a constant chatter in the ref's ear. But everyone does that. The Americans were working the ref. We were working her. I can't blame Abby or her teammates for doing it.

We're a physical team, and the teams we face always complain about that to the referees. I remember there was one instance in that match involving Carli Lloyd's head and the bottom of someone's boot. (Not mine.)

But that six-second call came out of nowhere. We were all in shock. *What? You're calling what?*

I guess I could understand it if Erin had been warned. Usually, officials do a decent job of communicating with players. I've heard refs tell goalkeepers to speed it up all the time. But I'd never seen six seconds called, and I'd never seen it called so fast and without a warning.

So the Americans got a free kick, and then the ref made a second call on a handball, which was almost more baffling to me.

Before every tournament we have meetings with the officials to go over the rules. Every World Cup, every Olympics, every qualifying tournament, you talk about what's a handball, what's a penalty, and what's not. We always ask.

Buddy—our nickname for Marie-Ève Nault—had her arm up against her body, protecting herself, when the ball, kicked by a US player, deflected off it. That's allowed. We were all in total disbelief when the ref called it a handball. Once again, where was VAR when we needed it?

Those two calls weren't fouls. They weren't side tackles from behind, or something else egregious. They were judgment calls by the ref. And they both went against us.

I don't think that referee has officiated at a FIFA game since.

In the moment, I thought, *Not only do we have to play the number-one-ranked team in the world, but we have to play against the ref, too.* But even so, I kept thinking we'd be okay. *Let's go—we'll just have to score again.* Obviously, we felt a lot of anger towards the officials, but you can't cross a line on the field. We just had to go out and win the match again.

We went to extra time, and it was just a battle. And then, of course, the US scored the winning goal on the last kick of the game.

You're aware of time in a moment like that. You can see the clock. But even though there were only fifteen seconds left, I kept thinking that we could somehow get an answering goal.

It was so deflating to hear those final whistles. It's one thing to have the victory taken from you the way it was.

It's another thing to lose the game on the last kick, when you're that close to going to penalties.

I'm not saying we would've won if it had gone to penalty kicks—who knows? But to be that close was . . . ugh.

When I heard the referee's whistles to end the game, I crumpled to the ground. I was exhausted. I was so sad, and so angry. We had lost a chance to play for a gold medal.

I have never been as angry as I felt in that moment. I was heartbroken. You'd almost rather get played off the park. That would hurt, but at least you'd know that you didn't deserve to win. Whereas that semifinal in London? I really think we should have won.

A lot happened after the match. And I think there was a lot of misunderstanding.

We came together as a team on the pitch. Peter Montopoli, who was the general secretary of the CSA, was there with John. Tanc and I were fuming. When we get together and we're both mad, we fuel each other. I remember Peter saying if anyone got fined, the CSA would pay for it.

One of the unique things about the Olympics is that before you go to the locker room after a match, you have to talk to the media in what they call a "mixed zone." There's no better place to be when you win and no worse place to be when you lose. When I was asked about the ref in those interviews, I didn't care what FIFA would think.

I wanted to be honest. I said that I thought the game had been stolen from us.

A lot of people believe I was suspended for saying that. I wasn't. I was suspended for the run-in that I had with the ref afterwards, on the way to the team bus.

After we had done our interviews, we went back to the locker room and showered and changed. We were devastated. We were destroyed. I've never seen a team so deflated. It was worse than the World Cup in 2011, because this time we felt we'd been robbed. We'd deserved to win that game, or at least deserved to go to PKs. It just seemed so unfair.

No one was talking. Everyone was sulking. Fun times!

I don't usually say a lot in the locker room. But this time, I did.

I told them that I'd never been prouder to play with our team, that it had been an honour to battle with them for that entire game. I remember saying that if someone had told us heading into the Olympics that we'd be playing for a bronze medal, we would've taken it in a heartbeat. That was our goal: to see our flag rise, to get on the podium. We still had a chance to do that. We still had a chance to achieve our goals. As heavy and as hard as it was in that moment, we had another game in two days.

I said, "I'm not leaving without an Olympic medal. So, let's go."

We filed out of the locker room. And then, as we were walking to the bus, we happened to cross paths with the ref. And I told her, "You were fucking horrible."

I swear to God, that's what I said.

Should I have said it?

No.

But the ref filed a complaint with FIFA saying that I had called her a "fucking whore."

Her English was not great, so I don't know if that's really what she thought she heard, but I would never call someone that. My teammates, my family, everyone who knows me knows that I would never say that. It's a word I would never use. If I was going to call her something, I wouldn't call her that; I would call her fucking horrible. Which I did.

That was the whole exchange. I got suspended four games because it ended up being my word against hers, and FIFA will always back their referees.

After we got back to the hotel, the team had a late dinner. Then I tried to go to sleep, but I couldn't.

The next day, John was the one who told me that I was under investigation for what had happened with the ref after the game. He said there was a chance I wouldn't be able to play in the bronze medal match. That was the worst-case scenario.

The team staff assured me that FIFA wasn't going to take any kind of action right away, because there was no such thing as a quick turnaround in a "she said, she said" case. It wasn't like when there's video evidence of a bad tackle.

But, still, there was at least a slight chance that I would be suspended right away.

I don't think the staff ever told the team what was going on. Maybe they were confident that everything would be fine, or maybe they didn't want it to be another distraction.

When you're in the Olympic bubble, you don't have a real picture of what's happening back home aside from talking to family. Also, as I've said, we do a pretty good job of staying off social media, staying off websites. If you choose to read something or look at something, that's fine, but you're not allowed to share it with teammates, unless a teammate asks to see it.

It wasn't until the next day, when we had training and a media availability, that we found out the whole country of Canada was in an uproar.

The first clue was that there was a lot more media there for us than usual. They kept asking questions about whether we had seen what was taking place back home. We hadn't, but when I talked to my family later, they told me that everyone was going crazy, that they'd never seen a response to a sporting event like that. Everyone was saying that we were cheated. It was kind of wild.

John is very good in pre-game meetings. He knows how to really get to you. To add to that, the staff put together a video with quotes from famous Canadians talking about the match over admittedly sappy music. Steve Nash and Wayne Gretzky said they'd go to war any day with our group. There was even a message from the prime minister. That's when it really kicked in for us that everyone in Canada had seen what happened and they were all behind us.

I tried my best to maintain a fine balance between understanding that we had not achieved anything yet and knowing that we had sparked such support and outrage within our country. When I'm in the middle of a tournament, I'm one of those people who doesn't read what anyone outside our bubble has to say about us. But it was hard to do that when I was getting messages from the most famous of famous Canadians, saying that they had my back. I did my best to block it all out, but it was almost impossible.

And we still had a game to prepare for that could put us on the podium.

We stayed in the same hotel as the Americans in Manchester, and I remember running into their goalkeeper coach, who had worked for Canada under Even. He reinforced what I already knew, saying, "You guys need to rebound. You have a chance to get a medal. You can't dwell on what just happened." That stuck with me.

By the time of the bronze medal match against France, I had gathered my confidence. I had just played one of my best games ever. I was ready to do it again. (I think there was also a little bit of remembering what France had done to us in the World Cup; revenge can be sweet.) But we were fried. We were absolutely exhausted. We had been riding the biggest roller coaster of emotions over the past three days, and a bronze-medal game is always hard to get up for. It's tough to rebound after you've just lost the chance to play for gold.

When the game kicked off, we just couldn't move. I remember thinking, *Holy crap, we're in so much trouble here.* France were so good, and we were so tired.

Rhian tells a story about passing the ball to me in that game. It was only a yard way from me, but I couldn't physically get to it—that's how tired I was. Carmelina Moscato was yelling from the back, trying to bring everyone together: "Defend! Defend!"

I don't know how we didn't lose. I really don't. But I guess there are moments when the good guys, who have suffered so many trials, somehow finally win. It was like we had a force field in front of our goal. Erin McLeod played out of her mind. France hit the post, hit the crossbar, with Desi clearing the ball off the line.

Midway through the second half, and still 0–0, we started to feel like we were going to get an opportunity. You start to think that something's on your side, that it's going to be your day. It's a cliché you hear sports announcers use all the time: so long as they keep it close, the underdog has a chance. It's true. All you need is that one little thing to fight for, that one little opening.

And then came Diana's goal. I don't know how she had the energy to be there, or how Kaylyn Kyle was able to make the best move ever, diving out of the way to avoid the offside. We wouldn't have survived extra time. I think we would have fallen over and waved the white flag. But Diana scored, and I remember thinking, *How is this possible?*

There were only a couple of minutes left, and the ref called a foul against us. We were stalling, trying to delay France from taking the free kick as long as we could.

And then the ref came up to me and said, "Just let them take it. I'm blowing the whistle."

She did—and we all lost our minds. We'd won our Olympic medal.

To go from what had happened in the game against the US to that moment was an amazing feeling. It was almost like we were able to survive because of what we'd gone through against the Americans. (Though, if we'd won that one, we would have been riding a high into the gold-medal game!) One thing our team would never do was quit on each other. But it's also true that if France had put in an early goal, they would have rolled right over us.

I had friends on that French team. Maybe it's the Canadian in me, but I felt for them. They totally deserved to win bronze and would have done it if it weren't for our fight.

When I talked to my parents the day after the game, they told me that they couldn't spot me in any of the celebration photos or footage: *Where were you? What were you doing at the end of the game?*

The truth is, I just hit the ground. There were tears. I was on my knees. We had this belief that we would be on the podium, but it's a whole other thing to know you're getting an Olympic medal. And to do it in the way we did, with that group, was perfect. It was so ugly, and so not perfect, and that was our team to a tee. Grit and grime; that was us. We fought and battled and clawed. To this day, I still wonder if the goal would have counted if they had been using VAR. Kaylyn may well have been offside.

But you know what? I don't care.

11

"WHAT THE HECK DID YOU GUYS JUST DO?"

I live in Portland. I play for Portland. I love the fans, I love the Thorns' organization, and I love everything about the city. I love representing it.

But there's something kind of transcendent about playing for your country. I am a proud Canadian. I've got a maple leaf tattooed on my back. It was my dream to play for the national team. As soon as I understood that it was a possibility, I decided "I'm doing that." And then to be able to help make a change in the sport of soccer—to take the country from no one caring whether we did well or did poorly to going on that crazy ride at the London Olympics—that is something beyond my ability to describe.

As cheesy as it sounds, to finally win something with

that team meant everything to me. Some of the players on that team are my best friends to this day and will be my best friends forever. It's not that way with every team, but we genuinely like each other and enjoy spending time together. We were such a band of misfits. We'd seen each other through the highest of highs and the lowest of lows, in our professional lives and in our private lives.

In order to play for our country, we had missed weddings, missed our graduations, missed birthdays, missed the birth of family members.

Was it worth it? Heck, yeah, it was worth it. Even going through what we went through in 2011 was worth it if this was where we got.

We went back to our hotel in Coventry after the game to pack up our stuff. I remember sitting there on my bed thinking about what it all meant, about what was about to happen. We were going to Wembley Stadium to get our medals. We were going to be on the podium. Oh my God, it was really happening.

I called my brother, and he said, "What the heck did you guys just do?"

"I don't know," I said. "I honestly don't know."

That was the truth. I hadn't been able to process it yet.

We had the wildest, happiest bus ride to London, but we were completely unprepared for the celebration because we had never been in that position before. There was no champagne, nothing.

We got to Wembley in time to watch the second half of the final between the US and Japan. Then we were in the bowels of the stadium, getting ready to receive our bronze medals, and we had no idea how we were supposed to go about it. Karina LeBlanc wore number 1 on our team, so she was supposed to lead us. But, of the bunch of us, she's the least likely to listen to instructions or follow directions. When they were briefing her, she was probably too busy talking, so we had no idea where to go. We did it all wrong—and we didn't care.

As a soccer player and a soccer fan, it's extremely cool to walk out onto the grass at Wembley, even if I couldn't help but feel a little bitterness at seeing who was on the top of the podium. But to be fair, a bunch of the American players came up to me and congratulated me personally. It's not like we're enemies. You hate them/you love them. That's just how it is.

So many people comment on how heavy an Olympic medal is, and I too was amazed by that when it was placed around my neck. I looked at it in disbelief. Sophie, who was beside me, blew a kiss to the camera when she got hers, and I remember thinking I would have to do that next time.

But mostly I just remember feeling sheer joy. There aren't many times in your life when you set such a lofty goal and hit it. To stand there and see our flag rise was amazing.

In such situations, people say you win gold, you lose silver, and you win bronze. The Japanese team, who lost to the Americans in the final, were on the level of the podium just above us. They had won an Olympic medal, but they were devastated (like Brazil would be in 2016 and Sweden was in Tokyo). The US was happy with gold, we were happy with our bronze, but the Japanese players felt awful.

And then, right after we stepped off the podium, my teammates and I were all saying, *Next time, the American flag can't be above us.* That was already our mindset. We were already looking ahead. It was crazy.

Winning is contagious. Once you get a taste of it, it's the only option.

After the medal presentation, we returned to the London Olympic Village. The closing ceremonies were two days away, and the organizers told us we were welcome to stay—and we were ready to party. I remember we had to go to the broadcast centre right away to do an interview with Brian Williams, and we pounded McDonald's cheeseburgers on the ride over.

That was our celebratory dinner.

The whole Canadian Olympic broadcast newsroom gave us a standing ovation when we walked in. That was nice. And, of course, for all Canadians who watch the Games, Brian was the face of the Olympics. I remember as a kid sitting on the couch at home with my parents, watching him. And now, wait a second, I'm on with him! It was mind-blowing.

We were so tired. What a day. Winning in Coventry, driving to Wembley, getting our medals, coming back to the village, doing the interview as a team—it was fun and chaotic and a gong show all at once. We were all exhausted, and Brian was trying to do a serious interview. We just couldn't function.

We spent the next day experiencing the Olympics for the first time as medallists. We went to Canada House and Heineken House and celebrated there. We got to watch the men's gold-medal soccer game.

That night I went out with friends who had come to London for the Games. We were at this tiny little pub, and at eleven o'clock, the traditional closing time, they announced last call.

My friends said, "Show him your medal." It's the kind of thing I never do. But I did it.

"So, is it last call even for an Olympic medallist?" I asked.

We stayed in that pub until four in the morning, celebrating and talking to strangers about football.

The next morning, I got a phone call from Mark Tewksbury, who was Canada's chef de mission in London, asking if I would be the flag-bearer for the closing ceremonies. He warned me that it would involve doing some things that might take me away from some of our celebrations.

I didn't even have to think about it. Are you kidding? Let's do it.

I have to admit the actual experience was a little nerve-racking. A chaperone walks with you when you carry the flag to tell you where to go. I remember her saying to me: "Don't trip."

Thanks a lot.

I felt such a sense of pride, but I wished it could have been all twenty-two of us carrying the flag, especially when I got to my assigned place in the stadium afterwards and couldn't find my teammates. I thought for a little while that I was going to have to watch the closing ceremonies all by myself.

Thank God, we had those jean-jacket uniforms, the Canadian tuxedoes. That's how I finally spotted them.

I've described us as misfits. We were also total cheese-balls. We knew the Spice Girls were going to be performing, and that, being in the UK, they were going to direct their performance to the Royal Box. We decided we had to find out where it was, and then managed to find our way to the front of the stage so that we lined up with the royals watching from on high. The Spice Girls came out in a double-decker bus, which was fun. Then David Beckham appeared. The soccer gods were smiling.

My first concert ever was the Spice Girls, so I guess I was coming full circle. It was so much fun.

I love closing ceremonies. All the competitors have worked so hard until this moment, and now we can just let it all out and enjoy. There's no stress, there are no more expectations. You can sit or stand or do anything you want and just take it all in, celebrating with people from around the world. And it was an opportunity for those of us who didn't get to spend a lot of time in the village to mingle with other Canadian athletes.

After the closing ceremonies, the athletes' village is just one big world party. Everyone's celebrating. Our team tends to stick together in moments like that. I don't know what it would be like as an athlete in an individual sport. But when you are part of a team, the ultimate is being able to decompress with your teammates.

There were a bunch of times that night when I reminded myself to soak it all in. You don't want to forget those moments.

One person who wasn't there with us was John Herdman. I think he flew home to Vancouver the day after our last match.

John isn't much of a celebrator. He coaches because he loves it. He wants to get the most out of his players, and have an impact, and help change their lives. But when the job is done, he's immediately on to the next challenge, not to mention wanting to get home to spend time with his family.

The same thing happened at the Olympics in Rio. He was there, and then he was gone. We were surprised, but not in a bad way. That was just John stepping aside and letting us enjoy it, while he got down to the business of planning whatever came next.

John had been coaching us for less than a year at the time of the London Olympics. There was only so much tactically and technically he could achieve in those ten or eleven months. He concentrated on where he could have the greatest impact in the shortest amount of time. He made sure we were connected—organized on the field, close as individuals, showing the respect we had for each other.

John prides himself on building a team that will fight for each other. That's what we were and that's what we did.

Flying home, I was part of the crew who were going to land in Vancouver—Karina, Brittany Timko, Emily Zurrer.

It's pretty nice going through the airport in the host city after the Olympics. Everyone's relaxed, everyone's happy, including the volunteers. And an Olympic medal shows up when your bag is scanned.

"What's this in your backpack?"

Then they ask you to bring it out and there are lot of oh-my-Gods.

When we landed in Vancouver, an Air Canada staffer was waiting for us when we got off the plane. She welcomed us home, and then—I'll never forget this—she said, "Your lives are never going to be the same." In the moment, we didn't really understand what she meant.

First, she took us to pick up our bags, and then she told us we might want to freshen up a bit before we headed out the doors.

Then we discovered why: there were thousands of people waiting for us, all of them cheering.

I remember what it was like coming home after the 2011 World Cup. There was no crowd—just me and my duffle bag. I don't think my family even came to pick me up. I had to take a cab. (Kidding.)

In one sense, a crowd like that is the last thing you want to see after you've just flown from London to Vancouver and are totally wiped out. I think everyone I'd ever met in my life was there. But I have to say I soon got over feeling tired.

I got home to a big family celebration. It's one of the best memories I have of 2012. I couldn't have achieved what I had without my family, and it was so great to share the moment with them.

There must have been twenty-five of us at my grandparents' house. We ordered Chinese food and the delivery guy came and soon he was sitting at the party having a drink with us.

My younger niece was two at the time. There's a great picture of her with the medal.

There's also a picture of my grandmother giving me the biggest hug. And then there's one of my favourite photos of her. She is wearing a huge white T-shirt—my grandma, she was crazy—with a picture of an old woman playing soccer on it. On the front, it says "Kick It Like Grandma." You can also see she has two wineglasses going at the same time.

It was so fun.

—

I can honestly say my life hasn't been the same since London. I don't think any of my teammates' lives have been the same either. And I know the game in Canada hasn't been the same since. I remember thinking that the 2002 U-19 World Championship in Edmonton was a turning point, and it was. But since 2012, there's really been no turning back.

It's been an adjustment for me, because I'm so not comfortable with being a public person—and that was even more true back then. I understand it comes with the game, and with being a role model. My teammates and I had been waiting our entire careers to be visible, to have people care about our sport, and I understand what that requires.

I'm not saying it's torture. It's just that there are moments when it's uncomfortable. That summer after London, I went to the Pacific National Exhibition with my brother and my nieces, which turned out to be a mistake. We were only two weeks out from the Olympics and people surrounded us like I was part of the exhibition. There were other times when I was out with my nieces that it got crazy. These two little kids would be eating ice cream and I'd have to tell people to give them a little bit of space.

My nieces are older now and they understand it better: Auntie is good at soccer.

After those Olympics, I had opportunities to do some endorsement stuff. But I was fine. I was set. I was comfortable. I had a deal with Procter & Gamble, but nothing crazy. I know a lot of athletes would have used the month after the Games to do everything they could, but that's not me.

Instead, I went to my family's cabin on the Sunshine Coast near Sechelt with my brother and my sister-in-law and disappeared for a week. That's one of the places where I'm the most comfortable. I've become more used to being recognized, but to this day I would rather go home, go into my house and then see you at practice. That's just the way I am.

I'm writing about my life in soccer for all sorts of good reasons, but if I were to meet you, you'd find that I won't reveal too much of myself until I've spent time getting to know you. Soccer is my job, and it's also my escape and release. As far as I'm concerned, what people see of me on the field should be enough.

In truth, I don't want strangers to know me. If I were just some random person living in Portland, people wouldn't care about who I am. So why do people get so curious about what I do in my private life because I'm good at soccer?

Even as a kid, when you can be a real hero-worshipper, I really didn't care what sports personalities did outside of sports, or what actors did when they weren't performing. I still like to operate on the assumption that other people think like I do about it all. I would never go up to someone famous in a restaurant and say, "Can I get a picture?" I'm just not that person.

I have slowly learned to accept the attention that comes with what I do on a soccer pitch, and to understand that people do care about what I say and do because of my job as a professional athlete. But I have always sworn to protect my family. I was the one who chose my profession and what comes with it. My family didn't. I feel like it's my job to protect them—especially the young kids, my nieces. All my family members are reserved people. We are very proud of each other. We are very close. And we want to protect the people within our family.

For instance, it was an amazing experience for me to play in one of our Celebration Tour matches at BC Place in April 2022. A belated ceremony was also held, honouring me for setting the career goal-scoring record, and I brought my nieces onto the field with me. I wanted to do that, and I am sure they will remember it forever.

But after the game people were coming up to them saying, "Oh my God, you're Christine Sinclair's niece! Can I get a picture with you?" Imagine saying that to an eleven-year-old. That's my worst nightmare. They're just kids. They have nothing to do with what I've chosen to do.

In Portland, people sometimes recognize me, but I have my privacy, and that works for me, one hundred million percent. It's different in Canada, though. I understand that people's interest in me comes from a good place. People want to come out and watch us play because they care. Which underlines how important it is for my teammates and younger players to have a chance to play professionally in Canada someday.

But unless I need to make a public appearance, I try to avoid the attention. When I come to town I stay at my brother's house. The people in his neighbourhood know I'm there and respect my boundaries. But when I walk around downtown, there's a lot of staring, and the phones come out. It's just not my comfort zone.

Social media came into being during my playing career. Teammates of mine have taken to it, building their profile and their brand and attracting sponsorships. I do what is necessary for the sponsors and causes I support. But I don't think the public needs to know where I ate or if friends of mine are in town. I don't have any desire to share my personal life with strangers. Fans care about how I do on the soccer field, and that's legit. But off the field, I would never choose to tell anyone outside my circle of family and friends what I'm doing. That's so not me.

The media in Canada and in Portland figured out early that I was someone who was going to put up some barriers, that I was going to talk business and that's it. I made it clear that there were things I wasn't going to talk about, including my family, and now, for the most part, they know not to ask.

I'm fortunate to be part of a national team with press officers who help me out. Before every season and all our major tournaments, they meet with players and ask us what we are comfortable with and which questions we don't want to be asked, and do their best to protect us.

Also, the media in Canada and in Portland have been pretty kind. They're not out to stir the pot and create controversy. If I were a male soccer player on a big team in Europe that might be different. But here I can still live the kind of life I want, most of the time.

After the 2012 Olympics, a new women's professional league, the National Women's Soccer League, was started up. I had been super close to going to play for Paris Saint-Germain (PSG). I had an offer, and I was serious about signing. But then the rumours began about the birth of a new league in the United States that would have a team in Portland. Like I said, I am a homebody. Like I also said, Portland is a place where I can drop out of the spotlight if I want to—a safe haven where I can just live my life.

There was no way I wanted to be stuck in Paris if there was a team in Portland. So I turned PSG down. I'm still playing in Portland.

As for the future of the national team, our Olympics in London was the culmination of years of grinding effort and announced that Canada had joined the ranks of the world's best teams. It's a position we've maintained ever since, year after year after year. It was unexpected—except for those of us who were there. All major tournaments have their wild moments, but that one had a unique feel.

And we knew what was coming next. Canada was hosting the World Cup in 2015. There was momentum.

Some players were going to retire after 2012, and some were going to get cut before the next World Cup. But now we had a taste for winning. We wanted to see if we could do some more of it.

Very few players get to play in a World Cup during their careers, let alone a World Cup at home. In 2011, when we found out that Canada would be hosting the next one, it seemed such a long way in the future. But then London happened, and the 2015 World Cup became our next major tournament. The timing couldn't have been better for soccer in Canada. We were coming off the highest of highs in terms of the sport. People were paying attention and caring. The buildup was just insane, and interest snowballed as the tournament—set for June 6 to July 5, 2015—drew closer.

My friend Nadine Angerer, who played for Germany when the country hosted the 2011 World Cup, warned me about what was to come. She told me that it had been the hardest tournament she had ever gone through. I'm not sure I really understood what she meant until after Canada's World Cup was over. Until you experience playing as the host country's home team, there's no way to know what it's like.

Everyone on our team was excited, and we felt prepared. John mapped out every single detail. His number-one focus was winning our group. If we did that, we would be able to play all our knockout games in either Edmonton or Vancouver, right up to the final at BC Place, and we wouldn't have to travel too much. He and our staff had it down to a science—every last thing.

Before the opening match against China in Edmonton, the team went to Cancun for a training camp. We were put up in this amazing resort where we were able to escape family and friends and all the pressures of being about to play in Canada while getting ready for the journey we were about to go on.

We turned over every rock in our prep. The staff even brought in a new kind of heat training, where you swallowed a little pill-like thing with a thermometer built into it. Every pill had its own serial number, which the staff could track on a computer. You swallowed it a couple of hours before training so that it would be out of your stomach and into your digestive tract by the time training started. There, it could measure your core temperature, and it wouldn't be affected if you took a big slug of cold water. At the end of the day, you pooped the thing out.

The idea was to see how far you could be pushed on a hot day without having to worry about heat stroke. Interesting.

Six days before the first match, we flew to Edmonton from Cancun.

The scene was nuts on a level I had never experienced before. The expectations were so much greater than when I'd played in the U19 tournament in Edmonton when I was a kid. It felt to me like everyone in Canada was saying, "Christine is going to lead us to the World Cup!"

I admit that I really felt that pressure.

The last time most Canadians had tuned into our games was when they watched us play in London. The last they'd seen of us was us climbing onto the podium to claim our Olympic bronze medals after being screwed over by the ref against the Americans in the semifinal.

A lot of people seemed to assume that, this time, in a bigger tournament, Canada was going to win the whole thing, not understanding that there were at least eight teams that had an excellent chance to win the World Cup. It was never going to be a walk in the park.

There seems to be some kind of big controversy in advance of every World Cup or Olympics. In 2015, all the talk was about the fact that this would be the first World Cup played on artificial turf.

I was one of those who believed that it was a really bad idea. I understand that Canada was the only country to bid to host that 2015 World Cup, and that our bid was based on the matches being played on artificial turf because that's what was in place in our stadiums. None of the owners were willing to take on the cost of installing grass fields just for this one tournament. And the CSA certainly wasn't going to foot the bill.

But it was a joke. I don't want to blame the CSA. Well, maybe I do, when I consider the fact that they are co-hosting the men's World Cup in 2026. Those games won't be on artificial turf—they'll be on grass. No men's

World Cup match has ever been played on artificial turf.

I complained then and I will continue to complain until a men's World Cup game is played on artificial turf somewhere. All athletes should be treated equally. Period.

Despite my usual bout of pre-game nerves, one of my favourite moments in that tournament was walking out in front of the packed Commonwealth Stadium for our match against China. Artificial turf or not, I couldn't help but think, *Look at what we are doing. Look at what we are accomplishing. Look at how far we have come.* I was so proud of Canada.

Then the match started and, holy, it was tough and it was close. China was *really* good.

The game was scoreless heading into extra time, when we were awarded a penalty. Going into the match, I knew that if there was a PK, I would be taking it.

It's amazing the number of things that can go through your head in the span of fifteen seconds. As I started getting ready, I was feeling the weight of expectations— it felt like all of Canada wanted me to score so our team would succeed. But then my brain switched to the shot and where I wanted to put it, and how, worst-case scenario, I wanted at least to force the keeper to make a great save.

My stress level? Right up there. Opening game, tie game, a home World Cup, the ninety-first minute, putting your shot where you want to shoot it.

I hit it where I wanted to hit it. Thank God it went in.

I ran to John. That instant was like a huge sigh of relief for both of us. The tournament had started, he had his first victory, and I had helped the team win. We needed those three points if we were going to win our group, even take a shot at being one of the top two teams of the group rounds that made it through to the knockout games.

But it didn't get any easier. After China, we faced New Zealand and Holland. You can usually count on having at least one easy game in the group stage. In that tournament our "easy" game was supposed to be New Zealand. But in a lot of ways, they reminded us of us—the little guys trying to knock off the big guys. And there was the added element of John's history as New Zealand's head coach before he came to Canada.

We had the better chances, but they had opportunities they missed too, including putting a penalty kick off the crossbar. The game finished 0–0, and the point for that draw put us on top of our group with one match to play.

But it seemed that wasn't good enough for all the soccer experts watching us.

In a home World Cup, you can't escape the background noise. When we were doing poorly in Germany in 2011, we could go back to our hotel at night and turn on the television and tune out. Even if they were talking about the matches, it was in German. Your progress or lack thereof wasn't hitting you in the face everywhere you went.

Though we were playing well, there was no respite from the national expectations. Here we were on the way to winning our group and achieving what we wanted to achieve, and the soundtrack all around us was that Canada is underperforming, Canada isn't doing as well as expected. The women are not scoring goals.

Even people within the CSA were criticizing us. It was non-stop.

What more did people want from us? We would have loved to have won every game, but that just doesn't happen.

It wasn't the fans who were riding us—the fans were incredible. It was the media, and especially the soccer pundits. It felt like they were simply trying to break us down.

Suddenly, Nadine's comment from years before made all the sense in the world.

It got to the point where I told our CSA liaison that I was done talking to the media. I needed to protect myself and I also wanted to protect my teammates.

It was the first time in my career that I had bowed out completely like that. But it wasn't healthy for me to have to face that barrage every day. I am my own harshest critic. I don't need to hear more knocks and doubts from the people sitting in the press box critiquing our team.

After I said I was done, we started to rotate different players through our pre-game press conferences. It wasn't just me; no one wanted to do it.

One measure of how bad it was? When Ashley Lawrence scored early against Holland in our final group game, we ran over to the bench to celebrate with John. But he didn't even notice us. He was too busy looking into the stands to where the press was sitting and giving them a fist pump. He was angry, and he was making a point. The game finished in a 1–1 draw, meaning we had achieved our goal of winning the group, which underlined the point he was making.

It wasn't all as tense as that. There were moments in that World Cup that were incredible, and I had experiences I will never forget. Getting to play at home, getting to play at BC Place. Seeing my family between games and having everyone's friends and family come to our hotel after the matches. That was wonderful.

We stayed downtown when we played in Vancouver, and the energy in the city was palpable. You would walk down the street and see Canada signs and Canadian flags and so many people wearing Canada soccer jerseys. It felt like we were back to the same kind of energy we'd seen at the 2010 Winter Olympics, which Vancouver had hosted. Seeing all the young kids out on the streets and in the stands for games was amazing. Those were the times when it was so great to be part of a home World Cup and experience that special energy.

We beat Switzerland 1–0 in the Round of 16 and we were right on track. We had accomplished everything that we wanted to by that point. And with the US and Germany on the other side of the draw, it looked like we had a realistic path to the final. That was my dream scenario: playing the Americans for the World Cup in my hometown.

Next up was England in the quarterfinals.

Just before the World Cup we had won a friendly against them in Hamilton, Ontario. England is world-class, but they were also a team we had just beaten and knew we could beat again. It wasn't like tackling Germany or the US in this round.

We went into the match feeling incredibly confident.

And then what could go wrong went wrong. We had a player trip at the halfway line and they scored. They scored their second goal off a set piece—we never concede goals off set pieces. It seemed like they had only crossed into our half twice and yet they had managed to score both times. We were outplaying them, but they were up 2–0.

I remember feeling that we still had this. The crowd was behind us. I scored and made it 2–1. It seemed inevitable that we were going to get another goal.

But it just never came.

In the last ten or fifteen minutes, we all felt a sense of panic. We knew that if we didn't get a goal we were out of the tournament. It happens in soccer. You want to play quickly when you need a goal but you don't want to rush. And it's especially hard when you know what's coming if you don't score. The time goes by so fast when you're down and so slowly when you're winning.

I remember thinking that we were going to get a chance. All we needed was one chance. We were prepared for that moment. We had prepped with John for being down a goal in the last ten minutes of a game. We had ticked all the boxes and put in all the practice time.

We just couldn't score another goal.

And then, in an instant, it was over. Everything that we had worked for over the past four years was gone.

It was painful being on the field after the final whistle. Careers were ending that day. That was Karina LeBlanc's last game, for one. We felt we shouldn't have been done. We weren't ready to be done. We had more to offer in that tournament.

Also, it's one thing to lose in Europe, when you've only got a couple of people from back home to watch you. It's another thing to lose with all your friends and family in the stands. It's hard for them to see you so sad.

As an athlete I never prepare to lose, especially not the must-win matches. My mindset is that we are winning today. When you don't, it's tough.

My sister-in-law texted me that night. "Are you alright? I've never seen you that upset on the soccer field."

I stayed with family in Vancouver for a couple of days after the England match and then went back to Portland. I wanted nothing more to do with the tournament. I followed it just enough to see who was winning, but I didn't watch. It was just too hard.

In that moment it didn't feel like it, but looking back I can see we had a lot to take pride in. It wasn't like 2011 in Germany, where we'd just stunk the bed. We'd won our group, we packed stadiums and we inspired a generation of young Canadians. But when you get that far in a tournament, you can't help but think of all the "if onlys." Unless they win, everyone competing in a World Cup feels that way.

Also, given how the Americans performed in that tournament, I honestly don't know if we could have beaten them. The show they put on against Japan in the final was incredible.

The thought of the Americans winning the World Cup at BC Place was hard for me to swallow, but there's no question they deserved it.

12

ONE BIG EMOTIONAL BLUR

Loss and sacrifice in soccer feels like nothing at all when compared with the pain and suffering of people you love.

In 2015 and 2016, my mom ended up spending months in hospital because of complications from her MS. But she was still my biggest fan. Until it became physically impossible, she came out in her wheelchair to see me play. My parents were both at BC Place for the Olympic qualifiers and the World Cup.

On Christmas Eve in 2015, my dad was diagnosed with cancer. I was home for the holidays when we got the call—one you hope never to receive. I knew he hadn't been feeling well, and he had lost a lot of weight. It turned out he had stage 4 colon cancer. He only lasted four months.

I had always been Daddy's little girl. He was the one who drove me everywhere and made sure I was okay and

happy. My brother and I went with him to all the practices for the soccer teams he coached. I spent so many
evenings of my childhood with just him and my brother.

Dad was both the fun parent and the one I turned to if
I had an issue.

No, let me change that. If I had a really, really serious
issue I went to my mom. I knew she would handle it. But
for the day-to-day stuff, the little things, I always went
to Dad.

Watching him with Mom after her car accident had
been so inspiring. It wasn't easy on him, but he gave up
everything so he could take care of her.

I'll never forget the speech my brother gave at our
father's funeral. He talked about how Dad was my biggest
fan. He said the only time he had ever seen my father cry
over good news was when Dad found out that I was going
to be Canada's Olympic flag-bearer at the closing ceremonies in London.

My mom had been in hospital for months when Dad
passed away in April 2016. Both were in Burnaby hospital
at the same time. Looking back on those months, I honestly don't know how we survived it as a family.

Mom had had some surgery and then developed an infection out of nowhere that got really bad. She was in the ICU
when we got Dad's diagnosis, and he went into the hos-
pice section of the hospital almost immediately.

My brother and I would go to visit Dad in palliative care, and then walk up the stairs to see Mom in the ICU. We did that night after night.

We had a national team camp in Vancouver around that time. John and everyone associated with the team were so kind to me. They told me to let them know what my schedule was with my parents and they would build the camp around it. I told them I couldn't do anything in the evening because I had to be at the hospital.

I remember packing up food from our team dinners to bring to my parents because hospital food is a joke.

Dad was dying and Mom wasn't doing great in the ICU. I even said goodbye to her one night when I didn't think she was going to make it.

After she managed to recover from the infection, she didn't remember a lot about what had gone on. I was thankful for that. She was going through enough without having to deal with the blow-by-blow of my dad's cancer.

She remained pretty out of it for a long time after he died. When she finally started to get better, she would ask me, repeatedly, "What did Dad pass away from?" And of course she couldn't go home without him to lean on, and from them on she lived in a care home.

It was a strange time for my brother and me. I remember one of our aunts saying that she felt bad because we had lost a parent when we hadn't even lost a grandparent yet. She meant it in the kindest way. (My dad's parents had actually passed away by then, but we hadn't known them.)

What my aunt meant was that most people lose a grandparent first and can kind of learn how to grieve.

Honestly, my aunts and uncles were our saviours.

And my teammates, too.

They were all great, but I'm going to single out Rhian, Karina, Robyn, and Diana. Oh my God. They would show up on my brother's doorstep with dinner for our entire family. Rhian knit blankets to keep my parents cozy in hospital.

There have been—there are—some really good people in my life. The connections on the team extend so far beyond the soccer field. I don't know how my brother and I would have gotten through without our family and friends. And for me, thank God for soccer. I would deal with what was going on, and deal with it some more, and then I'd go for a run. I needed to blow off steam or I would have gone crazy. Soccer was my outlet. But soccer also wasn't everything.

It's amazing what you're able to get through when you have to. You can handle a lot as a human being, or at least you can when you've got a support system.

There have been some rough parts in my life. Life kind of kicks you in the teeth sometimes.

But overall, I feel I've been very lucky.

The CONCACAF qualifiers for the Rio de Janeiro Olympic Games were scheduled for Houston in February 2016. John was incredible. He had already lost his own father, and he drew from that experience to support me. *Be home as much as you can*, he said. *This is just a game.*

Come when you're ready. There was no added pressure, no added stress. But I can't pick out much in the way of detail from that time—it was one big emotional blur.

I do remember showing up five days late for our camp in Texas. We went to Holland to play a game, and I showed up four days late. For a stretch I just showed up to play games and that was it. The staff and the players allowed me to get ready in my own time, and I am forever grateful to them for that generosity and understanding.

I blew out my calf in the first game of that Olympic qualifying tournament. I remember thinking, *I'm so overwhelmed right now. Can't something go right?* Our physio told me that people don't usually pull their calves unless they are really fatigued at the end of a game or in extra time, or under a lot of stress. Calves are apparently a place where stress shows up in the body.

I pick the second reason. That was definitely the one.

But as much as I was struggling, our team had never been in a better place.

We went to Paris for our pre-Olympic camp and played matches against France and China. I can still remember the feeling. No joke—we thought we were going to Rio to win.

Our young teammates—Ashley Lawrence, Jessie Fleming, Kadeisha Buchanan—now were playing with a major tournament under their belts. We'd all left that World Cup hungry to succeed. Our Olympic motto was AFTA— All for the Anthem. We were going to hear our anthem played. Anything less was not good enough.

In Paris we worked hard. It was intense. But players and staff exuded a sense of joy that I don't think I had ever experienced from the team before.

I remember one funny moment, too. I had a one-on-one meeting with John to give him some feedback. I told him that the forwards needed to work on our shooting more in practice. We needed more reps—which, I said, is the way I had been training my whole career.

"Just because you do it doesn't mean it's good for you," he said. "Just because you smoke cigarettes doesn't mean it's good for you."

The next day at practice, Tanc and I showed up with cigarettes in our mouths.

John had his birthday during that camp, too, and we pied him and pranked him. It was such a good group. It was fun, it was light. It was also intense, but everyone was in a great mood and in a great place.

I love Brazil. I've been there a lot. But it isn't the safest place. We couldn't really leave our hotels or the Olympic Village, and very few friends and family came to Rio to support us. And, in the tradition of some disaster or controversy plaguing every major tournament, the media was obsessing over the news that mosquitoes in Brazil were carrying the Zika virus. As a health crisis, it had nothing on what was to come in Tokyo in 2021, but at the time Rio was the most restrictive Olympics I'd experienced. It most definitely was the farthest thing from London, where we had been able to go wherever we wanted. (Jumping ahead here, but the night after we won the bronze medal a few of us left our hotel to try to find some bubbly. We walked to the corner grocery store, and when we turned around there were three armed guards running after us to make sure we didn't get into any trouble.)

We knew we had a tough draw in the tournament. We joked that it was a "Group of Death." Australia, Zimbabwe and Germany: both Australia and Germany were ahead of us in the FIFA rankings.

In our opening game against Australia, Janine Beckie scored in the first twenty seconds. We were on fire. Then Shelina Zadorsky got a red card in the nineteenth minute and reality smacked us in the face. We were down to ten players for the rest of the match. But we defended like crazy, Steph Labbé made a bunch of great saves, Australia hit the crossbar, and I scored a late goal to put the game away.

We were good. We were so good.

In our second game we beat Zimbabwe 3–1. We were flying. That win meant that we had already qualified for the quarterfinals before our final group match against Germany.

Our camp was split as to whether we should try to beat Germany or not. Winning our group would put us on a harder path to get to where we wanted to go. If we won, we played France. If we lost, we played China. We would rather have played China than France. But that wasn't how our team was wired. We were going out there to win. We wanted to beat everyone.

Germany got an early goal on a penalty, but then Tanc carried the team on her shoulders, scoring twice.

We won the group. We had beaten the Asian champion, the African champion and the European champion.

And, as a reward, we got to play a great French team, though other than at the 2011 World Cup, they tended to be underachievers in tournaments. That game was a coin toss. Sophie Schmidt scored a banger in the second half, and we held on for the last twenty minutes, defending for our lives. We were not losing. They were not scoring. They were not coming back.

I'm not sure that's the best Canadian national team that I have ever been a part of, but those Rio games were the best roll we had ever been on. The truth is, you can prepare like crazy, but you still need some luck. We had opponents who hit posts and crossbars. But we legitimately felt like we could beat anyone in the world at that moment.

So we beat France, and on the same day the Americans lost to Sweden on penalties in their quarterfinal. They were out.

And then the semifinal happened.

Our present for beating all those great teams was to face Germany again. It was by far our worst performance of the tournament. Still, I've gone over the stats from that game. Based on all the indicators in our play, we could have and should have won. But they scored twice, and we couldn't buy a goal.

It's amazing how you can be on the highest of highs and then, smack—you run into a German wall.

Sometimes we get lost in our own stories. We forget the stories of our opponents. We were fighting to hear the anthem, but Germany also had a story to tell. They had never won Olympic gold, even though they had won the World Cup and a whole bunch of European championships. We weren't the only ones fighting for something bigger.

Germany went on to win the gold and it was a huge moment for them.

We felt much less anger after we lost to them than after we lost to the Americans in London. But it was the ultimate disappointment.

In London, most of the players were part of a group who had been together for a long time. We were all kind of feeling the same thing at the same time. But in Rio there were a bunch of younger players who had never been through it before, and they took it so hard. Kadeisha Buchanan felt responsible because Germany had scored on a PK after she committed a foul. She and the other younger players felt like they'd let the veteran players down.

A bunch of us tried to explain to them that the only reason we had a chance at winning was them. *They* were the difference makers. *They* were the ones bringing a new sense of athleticism and dynamism, combined with skill. No way should these young players be carrying our sadness and disappointment on their shoulders.

Just like in London in 2012, I spoke up, reminding the team that we still had a chance to win an Olympic medal—there was still something so big to fight for. It's important that you switch your focus to the next game as soon as possible, even if you have to fake it a little. We only had three days to get ready.

John did an incredible job of rallying the troops. He gave us a day to be sad and mad and upset, and then helped us regroup and get back to business.

The bronze-medal game was against Brazil, which helped with our motivation. We were going into the lion's den in front of all those intense Brazilian fans who are so passionate and knowledgeable about soccer. You couldn't ask for more in a bronze-medal match.

We felt like we were back to playing like us in that game. John had told Deanne Rose early in the tournament that she was going to be the one to win us a medal. He has these unique ways of predicting things. Until that game against Germany, she hadn't played much.

Deanne scored early and then assisted on my goal late in the game.

Of course, Brazil scored to make it 2–1, and what should have been an easy game had its panicky final ten minutes. They attacked and attacked and attacked and we defended and defended and defended.

But Brazil had gone into extra time in both the quarters and semis. We thought that physically we had the edge because they had played sixty more minutes than us in the past five days. Everyone is tired at that stage in a tournament, but we thought we were less tired than they were.

And, after London, John had learned to spread out our minutes. In Rio he did a good job of rotating players and making sure people got rest. We were definitely the fresher of the two teams and, at the end of that game, we played like it.

I remember the feeling of sheer joy when the ref blew the final whistles. It was wonderful to see my young teammates win their first Olympic medal and to witness how giddy they were compared with how devastated they had been three days earlier.

It was an emotional day for me, especially, because it came at the end of a long and difficult six months. It was special standing on the podium with a group of teammates who had done so much to support me.

After we got our medals, we went back to the locker room. Desiree Scott wears number 11, so we always sit beside each other. She turned to me, obviously disappointed.

"I'm looking at an Olympic medal and I'm mad because I know it should be a different colour," she said. We had come a long way. I'd never thought that a Canadian soccer player would be disappointed winning bronze.

In that moment Desi and I vowed that the next one would be different.

And five years later, in Tokyo, in the locker room before our game against the United States, we both remembered that conversation.

13

COUNTDOWN TO BREAKING A RECORD BEFORE IT BROKE ME

We knew that someday John would move on from the women's national team—likely headed for the men's game.

At the team camp we had in Spain, late in 2017, he gave no hint that anything was out of the ordinary. Everything was as it normally was. We left camp as we always left camp, looking way ahead to the 2019 World Cup in France and the 2020 Olympics in Tokyo. We were given our off-season training plans. Nothing had changed.

In January 2018, I was in Denver, finishing up a run on a track. I'd left my phone in my car. When I got back to it, I saw four missed calls from Robyn Gayle. She had also left a bunch of text messages.

"Hey, can you call me right away?"

"Can you call John right away?"

Sitting in the car reading those messages, I knew. *He's gone.*

I called John and he told me that he had taken the head coaching job with Canada's men's national team.

He admitted that this wasn't the way he had hoped to tell us the news, but someone had found out and the story was going to be leaked that night. He was trying to call as many players as he could before the news broke, to let us know in person.

Despite his efforts, a lot of the team ended up hearing the news on Twitter, which was rough. I think some of them have never gotten over that, though they are by no means blaming John.

The way it happened was a shock, but it wasn't a shock that it happened. John never hid what his long-term dreams were. I've never been mad at him for following them. But we were losing an amazing coach who'd pushed all of us to be our best, got the most out of everyone, and got the most out of our team. That was rough.

The way he explained the timing to me was that he was one bad result away from not getting this chance to move on. As a coach, you're only as good as your last result.

We were coming off the bronze medal in Rio and we were flying. I don't know the details of how the CSA and all that worked, but they offered him the job and John saw it as his opportunity to make the jump. It has certainly worked out for the men's team, and it has worked out for him.

But I do remember thinking, *Really, CSA? You're taking our head coach away from us in order to fix your men's team? Really? Why don't you go find someone else?*

Maybe this was wishful thinking, but I'd hoped John would take us through the World Cup in France and the Tokyo Olympics—even though I knew national team coaches don't stick around forever.

That night, players were calling, FaceTiming and Zooming each other. Among the veterans, there was a sense that John wouldn't have left us if he didn't think we were capable of handling things on our own. He wouldn't have left us if we were in a bad place. He was obviously trying to advance in his career, but we believed he wouldn't have left us if he thought we wouldn't be able to succeed without him.

Hands down, John Herdman is the most influential coach I have ever had. It's easy to say that because of the results we had under him, the successes we had in London and Rio. But he's so much more than just a coach. Those of us who were able to play for him through his whole time with the team have a lifelong mentor. John fuelled our passion and our curiosity. I learned something every day with John. He prides himself on creating students of the game.

He always says that he sees himself as a fixer. He enjoys coming in and helping people discover their passion and discover their "why." He certainly fixed a broken team and a bunch of broken individuals after the 2011 World Cup.

But his influence is so much deeper than that, and he should give himself a lot more credit. Yes, he can fix things, but he's not *just* a fixer. He is a coach who can take players to the absolute top.

Seeing John lead the men's team to qualify for the World Cup in Qatar has been a blast. As a soccer fan, as a Canadian, as someone who knows John so well, I watched the qualifying games unfold, noticing the tactical stuff—for instance, how they switched formations three times before the half—and thought, *Yeah, that's John.* He's doing the same things with the men that he did with us.

It's not just on the field. We have closer friendships with the men's players now than we did in the past, and they talk to us about their meetings with John. He's not reinventing the wheel over there. He's creating a culture where players fight for each other and work for each other and leave their egos at the door. He's so good at that. I've watched the Canadian men's team for years and years and years, and until now I'd never seen any passion from them. It just wasn't there. They would lose must-win games 8–1. They blamed their coaches and they blamed each other. There were great Canadian players who didn't want to play for Canada.

It's all changed. You can see the brotherhood they've formed. They're fighting for each other—literally fighting, after the game against Mexico in Edmonton. It's cool to see how John can always find something to unite a group and to help create an edge—that us-against-the-world mentality. Of course, he also has a lot of talent on the roster, and he has changed some of the players. But most of the players aren't different—they just seem like they are.

That's because of him.

When John told me he was leaving, he also told me that his assistant, Kenneth Heiner-Møller, was going to take the reins. I was so thankful for that. We'd experienced a coaching change that hadn't gone smoothly when Carolina came in. There is always a fear of the unknown. But we knew Kenneth and he knew us. He had been our assistant coach for a year and a half, joining us after five years as the head coach of the Danish women's national team.

Kenneth's soccer knowledge is off the charts. He has an amazing ability to see the game and understand how it can be played and how it should be played. He is also one of the kindest, gentlest people I've ever met, so I figured the transition would be smooth. Things might change a little bit, but it wasn't going to be a complete overhaul. Thank God for that.

Still, you don't know how someone is going to be as a head coach until you play for them. Our first camp with Kenneth was for the Algarve Cup in Portugal, and it was immediately obvious to us that he and John were more different in style and approach than we'd thought.

John's teams play a very structured game. He lays out the formations for his players and he is tactically strict. Whereas Kenneth, from the moment he took over, talked about himself as a players' coach; he had played soccer himself at a very high level. He understood the game as being more free-flowing. He still had tactics and structures and ideas, of course, but once the players were out there on the field, he felt they should read what they read and see what they see and think for themselves.

Our first game under Kenneth was against Sweden. Our coach took the restraints off, telling us to just go play.

It was utter chaos. It looked like we had never played soccer before. Everyone was on their own page and it simply didn't work. We were killed. We only ended up losing 3–1, but the score flattered us.

I remember talking to Kenneth afterwards and saying, "Okay, I think we'll get there, but this team needs some structure." He recognized the problem as well. We slowly evolved into a team that had structure and tactics but also let players play what they saw and felt. We'd started to get there by the time he left, but I'm not sure we ever would have fully evolved into the team he wanted us to be, even if he'd stayed.

Kenneth prided himself on possessing and keeping the ball. If you lost the ball, you were only letting the other team borrow it and had to make sure you took it back.

I would love to see him coach Barcelona; those men play the way he thinks the game should be being played. Nothing against our national women's team, but that's just not who we are, or how we play, or the type of players we have. We are not Barcelona.

The 2019 World Cup was our first—and, as it turned out, our only—major tournament with Kenneth as our coach. Heading in, I thought we were in a good place. We were healthy and we were playing well.

We went to Paris before the tournament to play a friendly against France that we lost by a goal. There were no red flags in terms of our performance.

I loved the experience of that World Cup. We were in a true footballing country, and for one of the first times in my career I felt as valued as I imagine men playing in their World Cup must feel. Everything was first-class—the way we were treated, the stadiums, the fans. It felt big. It felt special. In France they did it right. (Plus, just walking out on to the pitch at Parc des Princes, where Paris Saint-Germain plays their home games, was pretty cool.)

In our group games, we beat Cameroon and New Zealand, which was enough to get us through to the knockout stage. We lost a close match to Holland in our final group game, which meant we were matched against Sweden in the Round of 16.

We had played them earlier in the year and won on penalties, so we knew exactly the type of game it was going to be—tight.

We played fine. They played fine. There weren't that many chances.

In the second half, they scored what turned out to be the only goal of the game, and we panicked a bit and started to rush things. You need to pick up the pace a little bit, but you can't hurry, you can't rush. I think we started to rush, and things got out of hand.

It's hard to lose that way, and it's always hard to be knocked out of the World Cup. You're in the middle of it, you're looking ahead, and then, in an instant, it's all over.

It wasn't until we studied the stats that we were able to identify some of our issues. We were just not meant to play that possession-style game Kenneth believed in. While we led in possession, out of all the teams that got out of the group, we had the fewest shots on goal. That weird stat showed that we weren't playing to our strengths.

But it's also true that we lost a very close game against a very good team, and there are more and more very good teams in the women's soccer world every day. Looking ahead to the Tokyo Olympics, we were feeling the same way we felt after the 2015 World Cup and before Rio. There was no reason to panic. We had time to fix our mistakes. We'd be fine.

There was a little bit of concern after we went to Japan in the first FIFA international window later that fall. We really shouldn't have been there. After just settling back in with our professional teams, we were flying across the Pacific for what was supposed to be a dry run for the 2020 Olympics. It had been a long year for all of us. Looking back, it would have been a great opportunity to bring along some young players who hadn't played a lot and give them some experience. Instead, we went over there and lost 3–0. They played us off the park. That was a little bit of a "oh no" moment.

But in the next FIFA window, we went to China and we played well. That was more like it. We were back to us. We were fine.

I did have one piece of unfinished business.

Heading into the 2019 World Cup in France, I was close to breaking Abby Wambach's record of 184 career goals.

It's weird. I like to think of myself as the biggest team player. I will do anything to help my team win. I will play centre back if they ask me. I will play goalkeeper—I don't care. Yet when I'm put in as a forward my job is to score goals for my team. It's something I have always found easy. I'm not the type to beat five players and score—that's Marta. But if you give me a chance, I'm going to put it in the back of a net. That's me in a nutshell, and that's what I have made a living doing.

Since I was a kid, coaches have told me that I always seem to be where the ball bounces—whether it's a pass or a ricochet or the keeper making a save. I don't know why. I know I am a thinker on the pitch. I try to read things. I try to anticipate things. I spent a lot of time around the game as a kid, watching and learning and trying to understand it. If I had a chance to go to the park, I took a bag of balls with me and practised my shooting.

Being in front of the goal has never been a place of panic for me. Some players get in front of the goal and it's like they forget how to play soccer.

For me, it's clear. It's simple. The game slows down. I'm comfortable. Scoring has always come naturally. I honestly have no idea why. I'm sure there are people who have spent more time around the ball than me or taken more shots than me who haven't scored as many goals. All I know is that I found my calling and picked the right position in the right sport.

I spent a lot of years up front as a striker, but now, in Portland and for Canada, I play farther back, in more of an attacking midfield role. But if I get a chance, I am still going to put it in the net.

I have also been very fortunate to have been relatively healthy for most of what has been a long career. I have had teammates who weren't so lucky. It broke my heart watching what they had to go through with injuries that shortened their careers.

I have also been lucky to have been on a Canadian national team that has supported me and given me multiple opportunities and chances.

But with all that said, I have to say that the buildup to breaking the record—the countdown, all the attention that came with it—was so painful for me.

After I didn't break the record during the World Cup in France, the hype continued to grow, and what I had done so naturally for my entire career got harder. I was feeling the burden and the pressure. That's not ideal for scoring.

I love my teammates to death, but every time I'd score, they'd chant—"Ten more! Ten more!" Then, "Nine more! Nine more!" The media was asking me about it every time I did an interview.

It was a lot.

I was still one goal back of Abby's total when we began the CONCACAF Olympic qualifying tournament in January 2020. Our first match was against Saint Kitts and Nevis, one of the weakest teams in the region. Thank God we played them first.

If something is bothering me or if I am stressed to the limit or emotionally out of balance, I tend to pull my calf. It's my go-to stress injury. People think I'm crazy when I say that, but when my dad passed away, I pulled my calf. In practice after my mom passed away, I pulled my calf.

The day before our first game against Saint Kitts and Nevis, I pulled my calf.

The medical staff asked me if I wanted to play with the calf pull, just to try to get the record out of the way.

They didn't have to ask me twice.

Every time the ball went into the eighteen-yard box, my teammates passed it to me. I got the two goals I needed in the first half and let out the biggest sigh of relief. There is enough stress trying to qualify for the Olympics without the added pressure of trying to break a record.

Thank God it was over.

I have so much respect for Abby Wambach as a player. You don't score that many goals without being a world-class talent. We are very different players. She probably scored a hundred of her goals with her head, and I've maybe scored five that way.

I played against her so many times and, for the most part, her team always won. The US have handed me some of my hardest defeats as a soccer player. So I'm not going to lie: to have this one thing over Abby and the other American players of my time feels great. Canada is so used to being the underdog, the kid sister. I'm so proud of the fact that, right now, a Canadian holds the record for career goals scored.

Afterwards, Abby was very nice. She reached out and made a video for me. Mia Hamm congratulated me. So did Christine Lilley and so many of the players I had competed against for so long. Prime Minister Trudeau sent out a tweet.

The biggest thrill of all? Billie Jean King reached out to me.

One of the things I am experiencing more these days is women supporting women (once you take away how competitive we are on the field). Women are trying to grow the game and make it better, cheering and celebrating other players.

Our strong desire to win on the pitch doesn't always bring out the best in all of us. But at the end of the day, our focus now shifts to how can we build this amazing sport and elevate those in it.

14

GOLD. IT WASN'T PRETTY. IT WAS CLOSE. AND IT WAS SO US.

No matter their sterling qualities as coaches and the impact they both had on us, it wasn't John Herdman or Kenneth Heiner-Møller who led us to the gold-medal match at the Tokyo Olympics. That was Bev Priestman—and all of us, of course.

We all tried to prepare normally, because it's "just another game." We told ourselves that and our sports psychologist told us that. But it's not just another game. It's a once-in-a-lifetime opportunity to win an Olympic gold medal.

After beating the Americans in the semifinal, we travelled back to Tokyo and moved into the Olympic Village.

Bev and the staff gave us a whole day off just to experience it, which was nice since we couldn't leave and explore the city because of the COVID restrictions. I've always loved just walking around, taking photos, meeting other athletes, and all of that village stuff. It really makes you feel like an Olympian.

Once we were inside, the Tokyo version wasn't all that different from other Olympic Villages, except that everyone was wearing masks and there were fewer people. In past Olympics, your event might have ended on the second day, but you could stick around right through the closing ceremonies. But in this pandemic Games, once your competition was over, you had to move out and go home. The food hall was set up with plastic barriers between seats, but at least we were all together and we could sit wherever we wanted. We couldn't go anywhere else except for training and our events, but with only one day to kill, we were fine.

Then there was a big uproar about where and when our gold-medal game against Sweden would be played. It had originally been scheduled for 11 a.m. local time to satisfy NBC, the US broadcast-rights holder. They had assumed that the American team would be in the final and they'd wanted the game to air live in prime time back home.

But it was so hot and humid in Tokyo that the playing conditions would have been brutal, so there was a big push to get the time changed. Sweden was fighting for it, we were fighting for it. Both teams were fully supportive of switching it. We all just wanted to ensure a better match. But we didn't find out until the day before that they were rescheduling the gold medal match for nine o'clock at night and moving it to the massive stadium in Yokohama, which is where the final of the men's 2002 World Cup was played.

That stadium was an incredible venue. And it was going to be completely empty. No fans allowed in at all.

It's extra important to stick to your routine, individually and collectively, going into a big game. Keep doing what got you there. I tried to do everything like I always did it. I listened to my music. (I don't have a set playlist, just whatever Spotify puts on for the day, but at some point I do have to listen to Michael Jackson's "Man in the Mirror." That song was part of our game soundtrack when I played for University of Portland and it has stuck with me.) I did my usual little pre-game walk on the field, and then the team got together in the locker room. Nothing changed, other than that we had to pack our podium gear because we knew that, win or lose, we were going to be on the podium.

Bev did a good job in the buildup and just before the game. We had already achieved our goal: we *had* changed the colour of the medal. But she always said that we were going for gold, not silver. We had come this far. May as well finish the job.

At the same time, a bit of the pressure was off both teams going into this contest. Sweden had won silver in the Olympics before. They had been in that environment; they had experienced a gold-medal game. We hadn't, but the Americans were the hump that we had never been able to get over before. In some ways, that one had been the more stressful match.

Sweden was incredible in that entire tournament. As we prepared for the final, watching them and studying them, we knew it wasn't a fluke that they had beaten the Americans, too, and steamrolled the rest of the competition. They were peaking at the right time.

We came out in the first half and we could feel right away just how good they were. We did not play well, and they dominated us. In the moment, they felt overwhelming. Wave after wave after wave, and we just couldn't settle ourselves and play the way we'd been playing so far at the Games. They exploited things against us that other teams hadn't. Their forwards were just so athletic: every single one of them seemed six feet tall, fast and good with the ball. They weren't the same Swedish team we'd played in years past. It's not that we were awful; it's just that Sweden was so good.

They scored the first goal and then we just defended and defended, trying to hold on. I've been asked many times about that day. I always say that Sweden played a perfect game, except they did one thing wrong—they let us go into halftime down by only a goal. We had experienced being down one–nil at the half so many times; we knew we could come back from that score. One–nil is nothing in soccer. But two–nil—that's a mountain to climb.

The mood in our locker room at halftime was very calm, almost matter-of-fact. We knew we had to forget that the first half had ever happened and think about how we could build and improve. Bev took some time to show us clips of things in the first half that we hadn't noticed, opportunities that were available to us.

We came out a different team. We had the sense that we were going to get a chance to tie it (and thank God we did). We knew we had to play better than we had in the first half, but we were also thinking, *Man, we can only play better. We can't be much worse.*

And then, in the sixty-seventh minute, we got our chance.

Allysha Chapman played the ball in to me in the box. I took a touch as the Swedish defender went right through me. Everything happened fast, but it was obvious to me it was a penalty.

But the ref didn't call it. I remember sitting there on the turf in disbelief. I'm not a diver. I got taken out. The Swedish players yelled at me to get up and I did, and the game continued until the ball went out of play. That's when the referee got the signal to go back and look at it on VAR.

The ref went to the monitor, and our entire team gathered on the sideline. My teammates were asking me if I really thought it was a penalty. I had no doubt.

I support the use of VAR, and not just because it helped us in that match. Not one of the penalties called in our games in the Olympics—for us or against us—would have been called without VAR. Refs can only do so much. One set of eyes can't see everything that happens in the game. VAR gives them a chance to get it right.

I know some people don't like the VAR offside calls, which can be so close. But if someone's offside, they're offside. In soccer, games are won and lost by one goal all the time. And if a goal is two inches offside, it shouldn't count. I remember a time a few years back, in CONCACAF qualifying, when the US beat us 1–0 on a goal on which Alex Morgan was clearly standing offside. But it wasn't called and there was no VAR. There are actual rules, and we should do everything we can to follow them.

It was no surprise to me that the review confirmed the penalty. And it was no surprise to me that Jessie Fleming stepped up and buried the kick.

All right. Game on—and on and on and on for what felt like forever.

Sweden had the better of the chances after that. We cleared one off the line and they hit a post. But we held on through ninety minutes and into extra time. Both teams were absolutely gassed: each team had played six games in the span of two weeks in high temperatures and humidity.

It wasn't a surprise when I was subbed off late in the match. You can only run so much. When you're done, you're done. The national team has worked hard at developing the team's depth, and our staff has done all the research and learned that teams that are successful in tournaments are the ones that use their full rosters. You can't ask the same eleven players to play ninety, ninety, ninety, game after game. It's just impossible.

When I saw Jordyn Huitema standing on the sideline, I assumed it was me who was coming off—we play the same position and our other two forwards had already been subbed. I knew I had fought my fight, and I had all the confidence in the world in Jordyn—she would be able to add something different to the game.

My job changes as soon as I'm taken out. From that point on, I give the players on the field as much energy and support as possible. I do anything to help, including grabbing water for my teammates. There are only so many staff, so it's also up to the players to help each other out.

It's a lot more nerve-racking to watch than to play, because when you're on the field, not only do you have some control over what's happening, but you also don't have time to think about everything. On the sideline? No such luck. You notice and worry about everything.

Sweden had one more late chance to score. They missed the net on a header, and I remember thinking, *Thank God*.

And then, after extra time expired, it was on to a penalty shootout once again, this time for a gold medal. That's the worst, the absolute worst.

The emotions we all felt during that shootout were over the top. I still haven't been able to go back and watch it.

Sweden's first shot went off the post and out. Jessie stepped up and hit yet another perfect penalty, and it felt like we had it under control.

Then things went off the rails. Sweden made their second penalty kick. Ashley Lawrence had hers saved.

The shootout was tied 1–1.

Sweden made their third shot. Vanessa Gilles hit hers off the crossbar: 2–1 Sweden.

Steph Labbé, who was smiling all the while and almost dancing along her line, made a great save to stop the fourth Swedish shot. But then Adriana Leon's shot was saved by the Swedish keeper.

Desiree Scott was standing beside me on the sidelines. I'm so glad she was there. There are so many things you start thinking in a moment like that, such a huge range of emotions you go through. When you miss three penalties in a row in a shootout, chances are you're not winning. Together, she and I started trying to come to terms with that. *Hey, silver's not so bad. Silver's actually really good. It's better than bronze. We achieved our goal. We changed the colour of the medal.*

If Sweden converted their fifth penalty, they would win the shootout and the gold medal. Their captain, Caroline Seger, stepped up to take it. I'd played with Caroline for two years and had lived with her in New York. She is a good friend of mine. I remember thinking, *Caroline's clutch. There's no way she's going to miss this. She's one of the best players in the world and has been for so long. This is her moment.*

And then she launched her shot over the bar. Honestly, my heart still hurts for her.

To keep the shootout going, Deanne Rose still had to make our fifth penalty kick. I remember Bev on the sideline saying, "God, I hope she has kept track of the score. I hope she knows she needs this."

Deanne buried it in the top-right corner, just barely under the bar.

(The next day I asked Deanne what was going through her head when she took the shot. "God took over," she said. Perfect. I'll take that . . .)

Now we were into sudden death. Sweden's sixth shot was weak, and Steph saved it fairly easily.

Our next shooter was Julia Grosso.

Julia is from BC, like me. I've spent a lot of time with her in training, in the off-season, watching her grow and develop. I loved that she was having this moment.

The Swedish keeper guessed right, and she got a piece of the ball. Nine times out of ten she would save that shot.

But somehow the ball snuck in. The rest is a blur.

Sometimes, the good guys win.

Suddenly, no one was tired anymore. I think our sprint to the on-field celebration was the fastest we ran in the whole tournament.

Nothing in my career compares to that feeling. We have won big games to qualify for things, and those are stressful, because you're trying to get into a tournament. We celebrate when we succeed, but that's not like an Olympic medal win. Neither is winning a professional championship or a college championship. Nothing compares to winning an Olympic gold medal—never mind the way we did it, in the most nail-biting shootout ever.

Very few people get a chance to achieve their dream. That day, we all did, and we did it together.

It wasn't pretty. It was close. And it was so us. We ground it out and won in the only way we could.

We all jumped into a massive dogpile in the middle of the field. There were so many tears and hugs, so many exclamations of "Oh my God, we actually did it!"

I hugged Robyn Gayle and Melissa Tancredi, who were staff by then but were on the team with me for years. It was amazing to be able to share a moment like that with them.

The Swedish goalkeeper punted the ball into the air after Julia's shot went in. When I saw that ball, I grabbed it.

I still have the gold medal ball. It's my baby.

Then it was podium time. Because of COVID protocols, we weren't allowed to go back into our locker room to change, so we had to do it in the middle of the field where everyone could see. We obviously hadn't showered, and the podium gear was so heavy it felt like it was made of wool. We were all a hot mess. But we didn't care. We had just won a gold medal.

Players were calling their friends and family and FaceTiming. I FaceTimed my two nieces. They were in tears and I was in tears.

Years ago, they had each given me a toy and asked me to take them on all my trips and photograph them on location wherever I go. My younger niece gave me one of her little PAW Patrol dogs, an inch and half tall. And my elder niece gave me what's called a Shopkin: a little plastic head of lettuce with a face, called Kris P Lettuce.

Those toys have been to the top of the Eiffel Tower. They've been to the Olympics in Rio. In London, I put them in my pocket and took them up on the podium. And now I have pictures of those stupid toys with me and the gold medal from Tokyo. It was just hilarious.

We lined up to get our medals—us, and Sweden, and the Americans, who had won bronze. I admit that seeing the US team on that third step was fun. But I wasn't going to spend my time thinking about them. This was about us.

Because of the pandemic, we had to put our gold medals on each other. Desiree Scott was standing beside me. The lady with the tray of medals came, and the one for Des was the last medal on that tray. I could see that it was dented and scratched. "Des, I'm so sorry," I told her as I hung it around her neck.

It turned out that a worker had dropped our tray of medals, and six of them were all dinged and scratched. (Eventually, they were replaced.)

Then we were standing on the podium hearing "O Canada." That's a moment I'll never forget. That was the cherry on top of my whole career, my whole life. And when they raised the flags, there was our maple leaf above them all. Okay, that was cool.

I thought of all the people who had played before us, who built this program, who got it off the ground and fought to have it supported (kind of, anyway). We wouldn't have been there without all of them—the Charmaine Hoopers and the Silvana Burtinis and the Andrea Neils.

In that moment, I also thought of my family, and all my teammates through the years, and all the staff, too. That gold medal really was the culmination of so much work and so many sacrifices and so much time.

We finally did it.

We had to do a lot of media after the match. Media is fun when you've won, so that was fine. Then I did a press conference on my own that took forever. By the time I got back to the locker room, the team was waiting for me so we could open the champagne together. (We came prepared this time.) After the champagne, we hopped on the bus back to the Olympic Village. It was a party for exhausted people. We were all kind of delirious.

It was one in the morning when we reached the village. But we continued celebrating until the sun came up. I think some of our staff might have ended up in the fountain.

One of the highlights of finishing an Olympic tournament is that once you're done, all the food in the village is fair game. You can have fried chicken and burgers for breakfast if you want to. For the next couple of days, I don't think I ate anything green at all.

None of our friends and family were in Japan, and most of the other Canadians had gone home because of COVID rules, so we celebrated with our staff as a team.

We were allowed to stay for forty-eight hours after our final match, and, luckily for us, the closing ceremonies fell within that window. We spent another full day in celebration, and then it was time to get ready to march in the ceremonies. (Why were jean jackets part of our team uniform when everyone knew it was going to be forty degrees in Tokyo?)

The closing ceremonies are always a blast. The athletes can all let go, since the stress is done. All those months or years or a lifetime of prep: finally, you can just relax.

But it was even better this time because we had won.

A bunch of us found a spot on the grass where we sat and watched the show and took silly photos and enjoyed ourselves. We stayed till the very end, to the point where we were just about the last ones to leave the stadium. We even managed to get up on the stage in the middle of the stadium to take photos. It was a last Olympic team effort: to milk these moments for all we could.

This time, I didn't fly home through Vancouver. I flew directly to Seattle, spent a couple of days at home in Portland and then drove up to Canada.

My brother and some of my friends threw a surprise party in my aunt's backyard. It was like a flashback to the big party my family threw at my grandparents' house after the London Olympics. I admit we broke all the COVID rules except for the one about holding your gatherings outside. There were probably fifty people there, but I hadn't seen some of my family for a year and a bit because of the pandemic. We were celebrating a gold medal, but we were also celebrating being together after not seeing each other in forever.

And, oh my God, there were people there from high school and people there from my youth soccer teams. Some of the people who'd supported me and helped me achieve what we did were there. It was great to be able to spend time with them.

The party lasted until about two in the morning.

The next day I visited my mom in the care home. That was during a time when some of the restrictions were relaxed for a couple of months, so my nieces and my brother and I all went to see her together. That was the best.

15

A WOMAN IN SPORT

There were a bunch of us who were set on retiring after the Olympics in Tokyo. For the last six years of my career, I have been battling a chronic Achilles tendon injury. At times it's been so bad it took all the fun out of soccer. If every step you take is painful, it's amazing how much you don't want to take a step.

Then, late in 2021, the pain went away. I felt like a new person out on the pitch, and I decided to push back my retirement plans.

After an extremely honest conversation, Bev and I agreed to take my participation with the national team month by month, camp by camp. She told me that Canada needed me to play in the next World Cup. I told her that I'd at least play the qualifiers in the summer of 2022, with the goal of playing in the World Cup in 2023 in Australia and New Zealand.

I really appreciate the way Bev has taken a lot of the stress off of me in terms of making decisions. We attack it together, which is very helpful for me.

As for the Olympics in Paris in 2024, that's a different conversation. I've had staff members for Canada try to persuade me to play. But who knows what's going to happen?

The Olympics are a different beast than the World Cup, especially for an older player. The roster is so small, and there are games every three days. I'd have to be in a really good place to commit to that.

I am not committing to anything, and I am not *not* committing to anything. I have goals and I have aspirations, but at this point I'm not willing to take the weight of the world on my shoulders.

But then I look at someone like the great Brazilian midfielder Miraildes Maciel Mota, known as Formiga, who just retired from international football at forty-three. She played in every Olympic tournament going back to 1996, in seven World Cups, and she's still playing for her club team in Brazil.

I'm not saying I want to do that—but it could happen.

I've always wanted to play at least a year on my pro club without having to worry about international football. The men do it regularly. They retire from their national teams and keep playing for their club. That intrigues me. Wondering if it would be possible to just be a regular player for a year has been in the back of my head.

I think I will know when it's time to retire. Steph Labbé told me she knew, after Tokyo, that it was time. She says she's been enjoying retirement—that it's been the best thing ever for her. I do know that when I decide to retire, I don't want the kind of farewell tour Steph had as part of the Celebration Tour. It was good for her, a fitting tribute, and she enjoyed it. But I don't want that at all. For me, that sounds like a nightmare.

I like the idea of how Tom Brady handled retiring (at least until he un-retired). Play in a World Cup or whatever and then send out an announcement saying, "I'm not coming back."

Whatever happens, I'll do things my way.

And then, once I retire, I think I'll travel the world for a year. But I might get bored with that quickly.

Definitely, I will stay involved in the game. Right now, I'm picturing an assistant coach's role. I want none of the stress and pressure that Rhian Wilkinson has as our head coach in Portland. Karina LeBlanc's job as general manager actually scares me. I would love to have an assistant coach's role where I could have a connection with and an impact on the players, but where all the responsibility isn't on my shoulders.

There's a chance that if I get into coaching, I will want control. Right now, though, I want to be able to work with forwards and teach them my ways, but not have the whole weight of the team on me.

And then there are other days when I look down the road and think, *Who cares about soccer?* Maybe I'll just open a sports bar, or maybe a doggie day care, and forget about the game.

It's not hard to imagine how my career would have been different if I had been a male at the same level in our sport. I know I would be a lot richer.

As a kid, I played for the love of the game. And then, when I was picked for the national team and played soccer in college, I bought into the whole idea that I was fortunate just to be able to play the sport I loved. I was happy just to be there. Happy to be living my dream, representing Canada and travelling the world.

I've evolved.

Now, if I hear someone say "Just be grateful that you get to play. Look at the opportunities you have," it makes me so angry. Would you ever say that to a guy?

I *am* still grateful to be here. I *am* still thankful to be playing.

But there's so much to fight for. There's so much injustice in the way we've been treated. Women in soccer won't stop fighting until there is 100 percent equality, starting at the grassroots level and going all the way to FIFA.

The fight is on.

I have a lot of respect for the players on the US women's national team, who sued their own federation for equal pay and, after a six-year-long battle, finally won. They showed what's possible, what's fair, and what shouldn't be tolerated. The federation had been trying to argue that women's soccer was not equal work compared to men's soccer.

Really? That's the position you're going take?

It's the exact same game. I dare you to say that the women who play it aren't worth what the men are worth.

Megan Rapinoe and I went to school together in Portland and were friends, but I'm just not capable of doing what players like her do, which is to get in front of the camera every chance they have to fight for women's sport and for equality. That's just not who I am. But there are times when you need the loud individuals to make noise, to bring the attention. Megan did that, and Abby Wambach did that. And Megan has said her fight is not just about the US women's national team but for something much bigger, which is helping to create across-the-board change when it comes to how women are valued.

I'm not a loud voice. I'm not the most public person. I don't want to be the one on camera making noise and being the spokesperson. But I will fight in the way I know how to fight. I'll do my fighting behind the scenes and work with our team and our lawyers. I will speak up when things need to be said. I will choose my words carefully and lead by example. That's how our Canadian women's team operates. We try to do things the right way and try to do things respectfully.

But there is a fight for equality that I'll keep fighting even after I'm done playing. We will fight until it's equal. We will fight for past players, current players and future players, and I will absolutely continue to fight in any way I can.

Seeing the US women win in court and then go on to strike a ground-breaking labour agreement with their federation that guarantees that players on the women's and men's teams receive equal compensation and share prize money gave the rest of us hope. I think it will be hard for a country like Canada, which prides itself on equality and the advancement of women, to ignore that precedent. The courts have forced the pace of change in the United States, but I believe the decision went that way because the general public in North America and some countries in Europe believe women deserve just as much as men.

Other countries have already started paying their men's and women's players equally. That's where the world is heading. But the Canadian Soccer Association is still not on board.

I have mixed feelings about the CSA. I have to give the association a lot of credit. They jumped into women's soccer and supported their women's program well before most countries did—including a lot of traditional soccer countries. They've done a lot to help grow the women's game and support female soccer in Canada. I give them credit for hosting the 2015 World Cup.

But funding and supporting a women's national team, and being proud that you do that, is no longer enough. How are you going to push the envelope? How are you going to create equality? How are you going to really support your women players?

The CSA's argument has always been that, unfortunately, the prize money for the women's game is just not going to be the same as for the men's. Yet I've been waiting my whole career for the Canadian men's national team to be successful.

I'm proud to be Canadian. As I write, I can't wait to watch our men in the 2022 World Cup. It will do tremendous things for the sport within Canada, as will co-hosting the men's World Cup in 2026. Soccer is going to take off, which will be great.

But there's the little selfish part of me that thinks maybe now is the time to show support to the team that has been carrying the CSA for years—my team. The women's team. You claimed you couldn't fund us as well as other countries funded their women's teams because our men's team wasn't successful. Well, how about now? It's time to show up and actually do it.

Our national team is operating five years behind the US women's team. Things they did five years ago are what we're trying to do now. I'm involved in that. I hope that it doesn't come to the point where we have to sue our association the way the American women sued theirs. But if we have to, we will. If we have to go down the same road in Canada and take the CSA to court, I think public opinion will be on our side.

But equal pay at the national team level is only the tip of the iceberg.

I'm a firm believer in the idea that a little girl should have every opportunity a little boy gets. I'm not talking about the opportunity to play here, because, in Canada, girls do have the opportunity to play. I'm talking about the advancement of girls and women in all parts of the sport.

Men routinely get the chance to manage teams with no previous coaching experience. The theory is that if you were a good player, you'll be a good coach. You never see that on the women's side. They'd rather hire a guy to coach over a female who has played at the highest level but might not have as much coaching experience. It's a double standard that exists throughout the sport.

And then there's the sexism of FIFA. They loved talking about how they increased the women's prize money at the last World Cup—and it's great that it was increased. But they increased the men's prize money by more, so the gap actually grew wider. We are farther behind.

For a long time, I've joked that I volunteered to play soccer for Canada.

Still, I've steadily played for professional teams too. I've been very fortunate compared to some of my team-mates who needed to work second jobs just to make ends meet. I've never had to do that. I've never had to have a job in my life besides playing soccer.

Financially, things changed after the London Olympics in 2012. People came out to watch every single game we played. People cared how we did and wanted to see us on TV. There were new opportunities for me in Canada—speaking engagements, endorsements. It adds up, but given the career I've had, if I were a guy I wouldn't be living in a little three-bedroom house.

The National Women's Soccer League was also formed on the back of those London Olympics, and it has turned out to be a game changer.

Establishing women's professional soccer in North America has been incredibly difficult.

When I was in college, a league called the Women's United Soccer Association was operating, and it featured a lot of the stars from the US national team. It folded just as I was graduating. I remember that being upsetting for me because I am a homebody. I never wanted to play overseas. It just never appealed to me. With WUSA gone, I didn't have a professional opportunity in North America.

Then I have experienced one league folding while I was part of it—the Women's Professional Soccer league, which was launched in 2010. I played in the Bay Area for FC Gold Pride. We won the championship in 2010 and then the team went under. The next season, I moved to the Western New York Flash in Buffalo. We won the championship—and then that team folded too. The whole league collapsed before the 2012 season.

At that point I was thinking maybe the United States wasn't ready for women's professional soccer. Maybe we just weren't there yet. But, two years later, the NWSL was formed, and I don't see it folding. I think it will be around forever. It just keeps growing and the standards keep getting better. It's been cool to be a part of its evolution.

I've been fortunate to play at home in Portland with the Thorns. The fans here have been very supportive from the start. In the first couple years of the NWSL we averaged more fans than half the Major League Soccer teams.

But not every player in the league has had the same luck and same good fortune that I have had. Some ended up playing on teams that went under. Some were on teams that had locker rooms in school portables and bathrooms in porta-potties.

Now that we've signed our first collective agreement with the league, there are standards that have to be met—and they are being met. The players feel they are being treated professionally. They have the right environment and the opportunity to succeed.

Things are moving in the right direction—but it's so slow. Players in the NWSL are signing million-dollar contracts now. That was unheard of even five years ago. It's no longer just the big one-off tournaments that people care about. The average attendance for NWSL games is almost ten thousand, and it's growing. Women's pro soccer is here to stay.

But that mostly benefits the best of the best. Not everyone's on a national team. Not everyone's participating in World Cups and earning bonuses. The minimum wage in the NWSL this year was $35,000. I'm sorry, but someone making $35,000 and having to live in New York is not that far above the poverty line.

We need to fight for everyone.

It's the same story for the professional leagues in Europe. In the French league, if you don't play for PSG or Lyon, you'll have a completely different life than the players on those big clubs.

And in England, it's only been during the past five years that people have started to give that league a shot. Now they're affiliated with the Premier League and some of the biggest men's clubs in the world. I can't imagine the players accepting lower standards than the men for too much longer. Women are fed up with being treated as second class. It's only a matter of time before everything changes.

It is already changing for the young players coming into the game now. The best of the best in North America don't go to college anymore. They go from high school directly to the pros. Girls can dream of turning professional, whereas when I was coming up, that wasn't a realistic option.

Today's young players don't know what it's like to have to fight for everything. I think of players like Charmaine Hooper, who stood up for women in Canada when national team players were making ten dollars a day. Today's players would never understand that. They know what they're worth. They know that they should be making money. They assume that because they're playing pro, there are going to be opportunities. That's how far the game has come. And I can only imagine what it will be like in another fifteen or twenty years: when players are coming through youth academies, when you sign with the

Portland Thorns at ten and then work your way through their system.

It's only a matter of time before that starts to happen for women athletes, the way it's already happened in the men's game.

But Canada needs to keep up.

The opportunity's there. Grassroots soccer and the player pipeline will benefit from all those eight-year-olds who are dreaming of playing for Canada one day. But John Herdman said it best: our female players are still making the national team by chance instead of on purpose. They happened to be seen by a coach when they had a good game and got called into a camp. The systems in place in the United States aren't perfect, but if you're good, you're going to get seen. In Canada, that's not always the case. There isn't a legitimate pathway to develop and progress from one level to the next to the next.

I was fortunate. Not everyone is like me, but that doesn't mean they shouldn't have a chance.

That's one of the reasons why we need a domestic professional women's league in Canada. We are the only country in the world's top twenty that doesn't have a professional environment for their females to play in. That just doesn't make sense to me. We're a progressive country. We pride ourselves on opportunities for all. But at times, it seems we're all talk.

Canada has a gold-medal-winning team. We qualify for all the big tournaments. If not now, when are we ever going to start a professional league?

Just having a couple of NWSL teams in Canada won't do it. If you have a team in Vancouver and a team in Toronto that's maybe twenty Canadian players taken care of. That's not changing the landscape of soccer within the country. That's still the national team players plus a couple more. You're not creating opportunities.

I believe in a Canadian league. I look at the NWSL and think of the number of players that would never have been on the US national team except for their performances there. The depth that team has now is absolutely insane.

But investors and governments in Canada still don't want to take a risk on women's sports. They are willing to risk losing millions of dollars on men's sports. But heaven forbid someone takes a risk on women.

I'm hugely grateful to all those Canadians who have supported the national team over the years. Thank you for having our backs. I think of the 2011 World Cup, when things went so badly, and people still cheered us on. Since then we've taken them on a journey. And through it all they have remained diehard fans.

But the progressive part of me wants those same people to get out and demand equality and demand opportunities for young girls. It doesn't have to be soccer. The inequalities are there in absolutely everything. I could go on about the pay gap in other jobs. I think of my two little nieces: they deserve every chance to be successful in life.

Soccer is just the tip of the iceberg. It's just something that people happen to watch on TV. The same scenario exists everywhere.

I've learned that sports gives an athlete like me a unique voice. For some reason, people listen: I don't know why, because there are much smarter and much more powerful individuals out there than me, making real differences in the world. But think about the US team and their lawsuit. They used their success on the field to create a movement off the field. That success is going to push other female sports to match it. And then maybe, if sports are doing it, other workplaces will do it too.

Sometimes I wonder what it would have been like if I were starting out as a player now. In terms of opportunities and standards, there's no question it would be better. Someone like Jordyn Huitema is never going to experience getting dressed in a portable classroom set up as a makeshift locker room. I can only imagine what opportunities would be there for me if I were graduating from high school in 2022.

That being said, I've loved every step of my journey. I loved going to college and winning there. I loved fighting the early battles on the national team. I loved playing for Canada and being a part of the change.

When I'm done playing, I will still be proud of our gold medal from Tokyo and those national championships at the University of Portland. But I think the thing I'll be most proud of is that I helped to change the sport. Not many people are able to say something like that. (Maybe I'll write into the next contract with the CSA that they have to keep paying for past service—even in retirement.)

I think back to 2012 in London. Our goal was to inspire a new generation of players. Now that next generation is playing for Canada. And those we inspired are going to inspire the next generation after them. It's a pretty cool cycle.

But if Canada doesn't create a professional league, we will get left behind. Other powerhouse soccer nations are starting to support their women's national teams and women's professional teams more than we do. I think about Spain, with the women's teams at Barcelona and Real Madrid, and about what's going on in France and England. Even Mexico has their own women's league now.

You can see the impact of these changes on the performance of women's youth teams: our U20s recently lost to Mexico. Ten years ago, we wouldn't have. There is a correlation there. If you support and invest, it will show in the outcomes.

Those countries have passed us by in their support of their female players, no doubt about it. In Canada, we do a very good job of producing amazing, talented players. But that's it. I fear that for every Ashley Lawrence coming up against the odds in Canada, five exciting players are rising in those other places, because in those countries every young girl is getting excellent coaching and exactly what they need. We're not doing that.

Women's soccer has changed so much over the past twenty years. It has grown by leaps and bounds. When I first joined the national team, there was a huge gap between the top teams and everyone else. If you were one of the top three or four teams in the world, you basically won it all. If you were in the middle tier—and for the longest time Canada was in that middle tier—you could beat teams in the third tier 6–0, but you were still likely to lose to the US by just as much.

Now the gap has closed almost completely. You still have countries that don't support their women's teams. But the teams qualifying for World Cups and the Olympics are all competitive. You head into major tournaments now and play six or eight teams realistically expecting to win. It's exciting to witness, for sure, but at the same time it decreases your chance of winning.

Back when I started it was the fittest, fastest and strongest team that would typically win, and that was usually the Americans. It was scary how many goals they would score in the last ten minutes of halves just because they were in better shape than everyone else.

Now everyone is just as fit as them. Everyone is just as fast and athletic. And the game is truly becoming what it should be.

You still need to be a great athlete, but you also have to be able to play with the ball at your feet. You need to be able to read the game and understand the game. The level of coaching and tactics have improved as well. You can no longer be successful if you just have one piece of the puzzle. Even some of the teams that are technically sound, like Japan, aren't winning consistently anymore because they are being physically dominated. You need to combine fitness and skill and tactics to succeed.

That's where the women's game is heading.

In Canada we assume that we will be fine. We assume that because we've been good at this, we will carry on being good. My fear is that we will soon be surpassed by countries that support their youth programs, support their national women's teams and also support professional women's leagues.

Given what I've done with my life so far, and how much the sport of soccer has given me and the other players I've been honoured to play with and against, that scares me.

POSTSCRIPT

These last words are for my mother, who tried so hard, for so long, to stay with us.

Breaking the scoring record seems a while ago now, way back before the pandemic. And back in those before times, in 2020, we had a plan to celebrate it when the team was scheduled to play a friendly against Australia at BC Place as part of our preparation for the Tokyo Olympics. There was going to be a ceremony before the match, and we were determined to find a way to get my mom there and get her on the field. She was so looking forward to it.

Then COVID hit. The match, the celebration—and just about everything else on the planet—was cancelled.

The ceremony was finally rescheduled for April 2022, as part of the national team's Celebration Tour. I was honoured for the goal-scoring record in a pre-game ceremony at BC Place before the first of two friendlies we were playing against Nigeria.

But my mother couldn't be there. She passed away on February 2, while I was writing this book.

It was extremely bittersweet to be missing her, and missing Dad, as one of the biggest accomplishments of my career was being recognized. They supported me every step of the way, and it would have been so cool to have been able to share it with them.

But it was also incredibly special to see almost my entire extended family come out to BC Place. Aunts and uncles, great-aunts and great-uncles, lots and lots of cousins. It was just insane how many of us were in the building.

Mom would have loved that in some weird way her passing brought an already close family even closer. I didn't think that was possible, but it happened. Our relatives have taken my brother and me under their wings and helped us get through a really crappy time over these past few months.

When I walked out into the stadium that night, I was able to look up into the stands and see my family there. I was so fortunate when it comes to my parents. I have the best family in the world. I know a lot of people say that, but in my case, it is absolutely true. They are the most supportive and loving group. I don't know where I would be without them.

The best part of that night was being able to bring my two nieces out with me onto the field. They are the most important people in my life. I would do anything for those two kids. I want to give them everything in the world.

My nieces know absolutely everything about me as a person. They know that I play soccer and that I happen to be good and that I play for Canada. But I love that they never seem to be swayed by all the fuss, even on a night like that.

When I'm with them and attract attention or draw a crowd, they always say the same thing. "If only those people knew the real you . . ."

ACKNOWLEDGEMENTS

I'd like to thank Stephen Brunt for helping me get my words and thoughts on the page. He made writing about myself almost easy. I'm grateful to my manager, Brian Levine, and literary agent Rick Broadhead for persuading me to do this book. It wasn't at the top of my bucket list after the Tokyo Olympics, but they reminded me how important it is to use my platform to effect change.

My thanks to the whole team at Random House Canada: publisher Sue Kuruvilla, my editor and the imprint's executive editor, Anne Collins, the book's designer, Matthew Flute, and the sales, marketing and publicity crew who worked so hard to get the word out.

My coaches and teammates over the years have my deep gratitude: without them, I really wouldn't have much to write about. I especially want to thank my fellow national team vets for their enduring friendship.

Lastly, my biggest thanks to my entire family, and especially my brother and sister-in-law and my nieces for being who they are. Without them, my life would be so much less.

INDEX

CHRISTINE SINCLAIR is the long-time forward and captain of Canada's national soccer team and the Portland Thorns FC of the National Women's Soccer League. An Olympic gold medallist, two-time Olympic bronze medallist, CONCACAF champion, and fourteen-time winner of the Canadian Soccer Player of the Year award, and only the second player ever to appear and score in five FIFA Women's World Cups, Sinclair has scored 190 goals in international competition, more than any other player of any gender in history. Sinclair has also played in more than 310 international games in her professional football career, the most appearances by any active women's player. In 2022, she was the recipient of the inaugural The Best FIFA Special Award for women's football in recognition of her record-breaking goal scoring. Born and raised in Burnaby, BC, she currently lives in Portland, Oregon.

STEPHEN BRUNT is an award-winning writer and broadcaster with Rogers Sportsnet and the author of many bestselling books including *Facing Ali*; *Searching for Bobby Orr*; and *Gretzky's Tears*. Two of his most recent books are Jordin Tootoo's *All the Way* and the hockey memoir from Brian Burke, *Burke's Law,* which became a #1 bestseller. He is the co-founder and artistic director of the Writers at Woody Point festival, and divides his time between Hamilton, Ontario, where he was born, and Newfoundland.